Georg Gatsas
Five Points

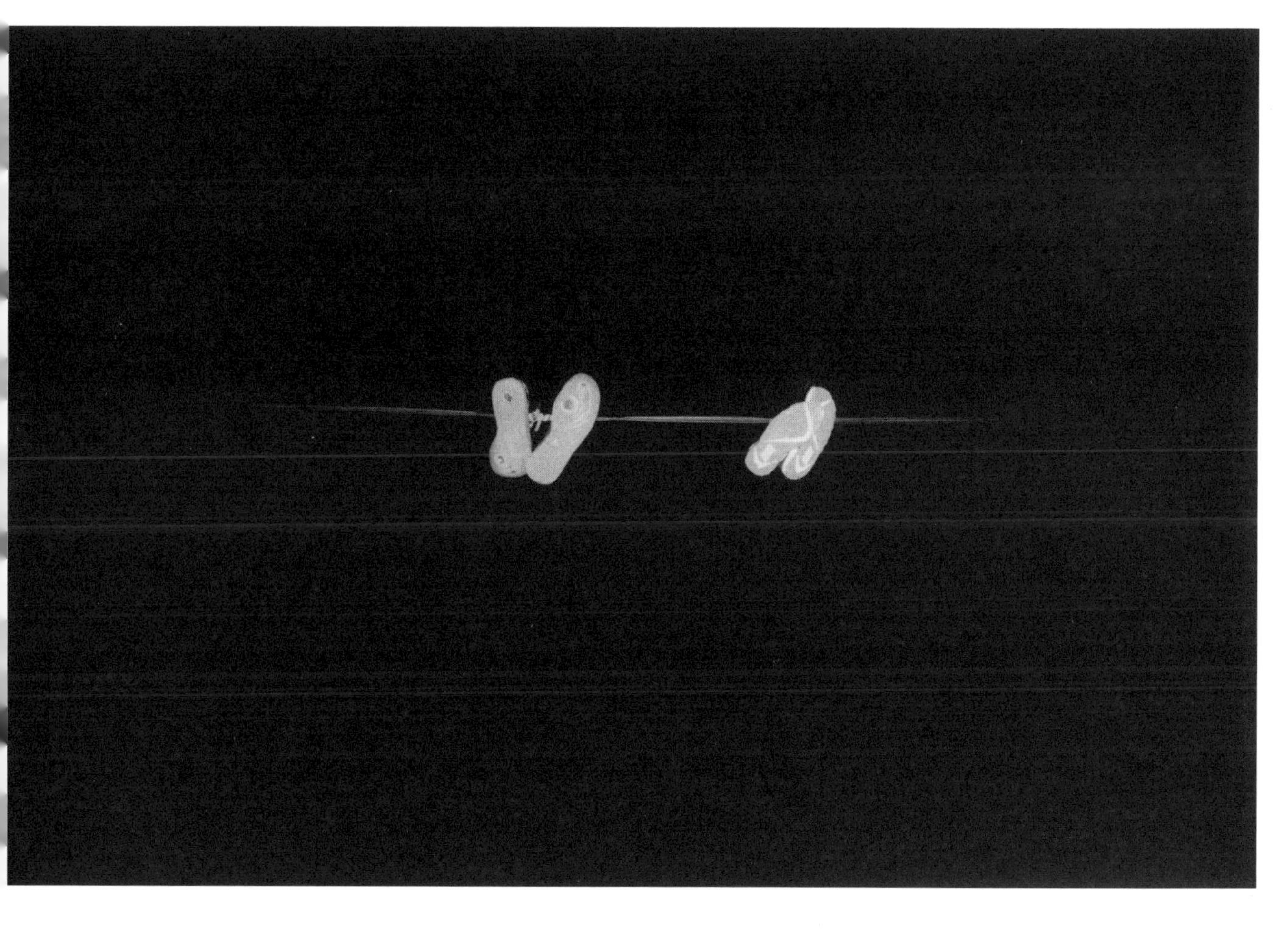

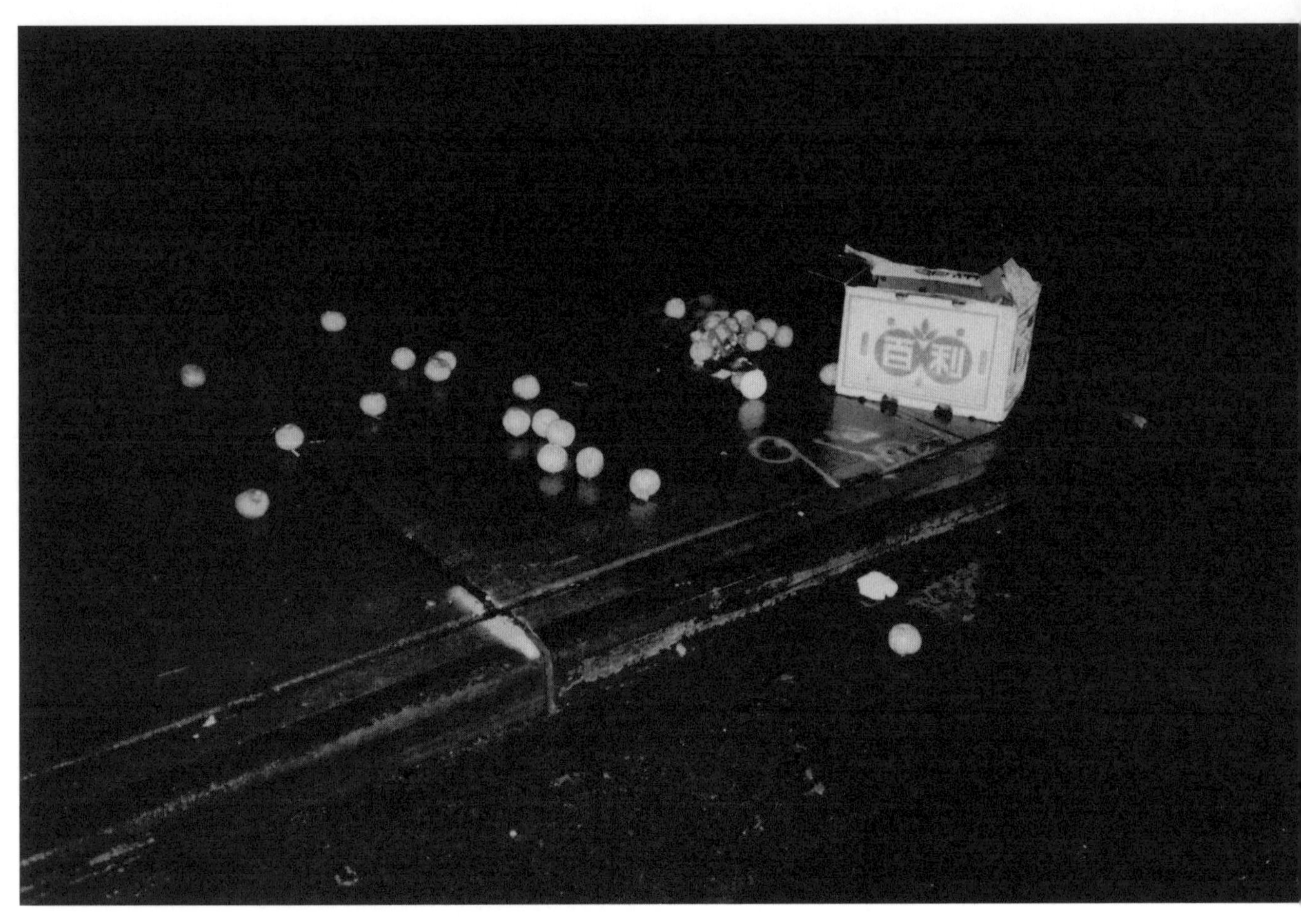
百利

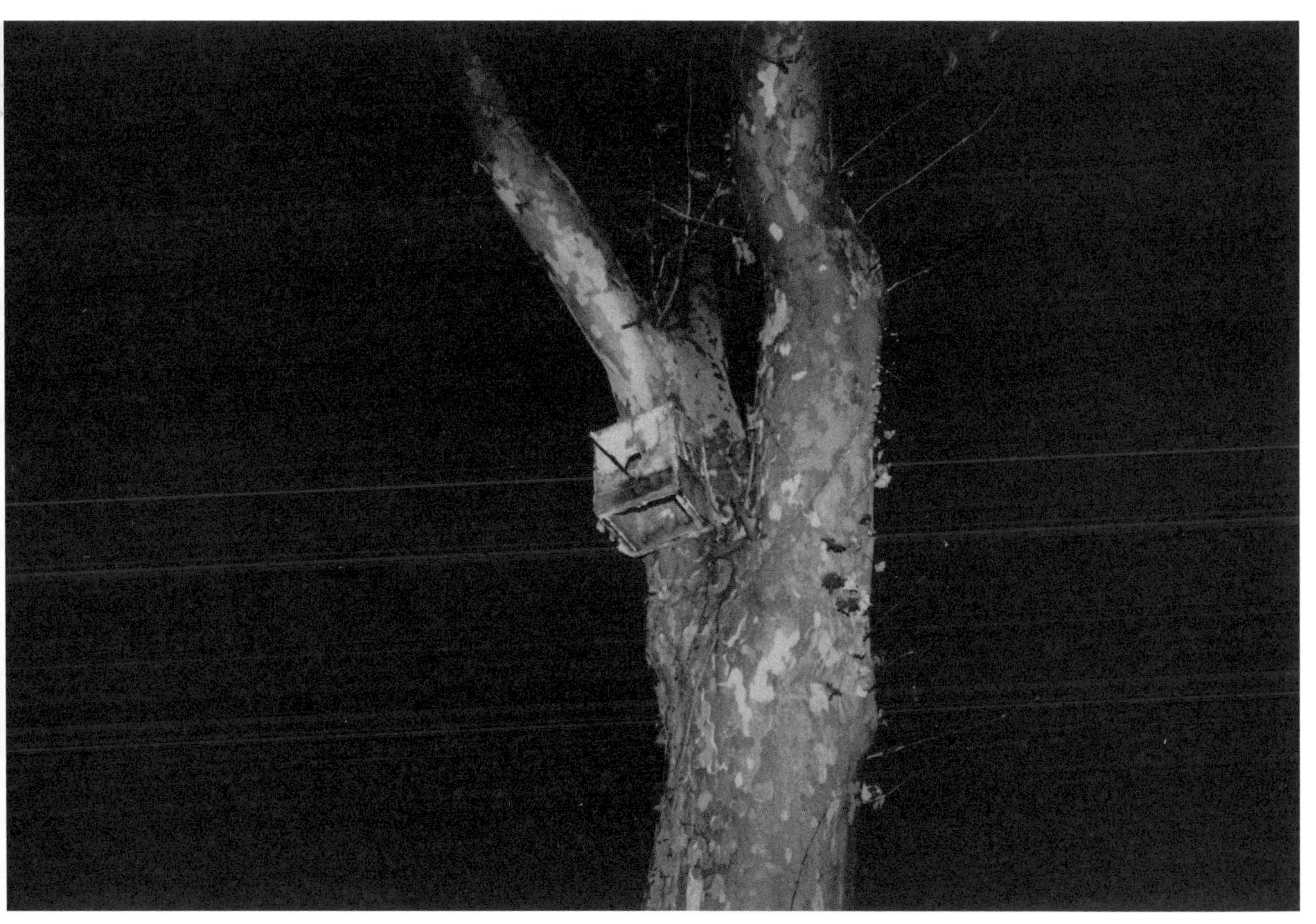

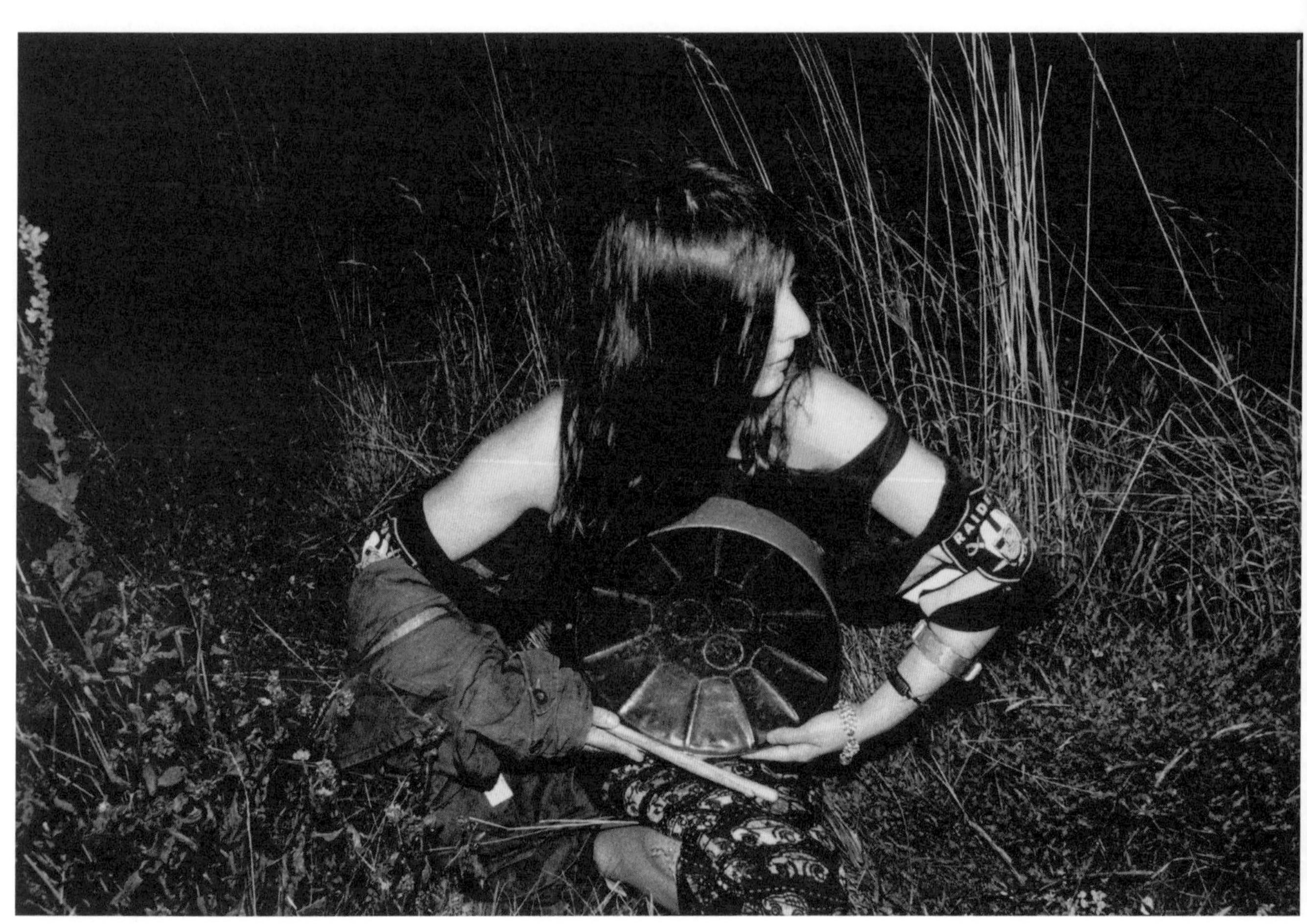

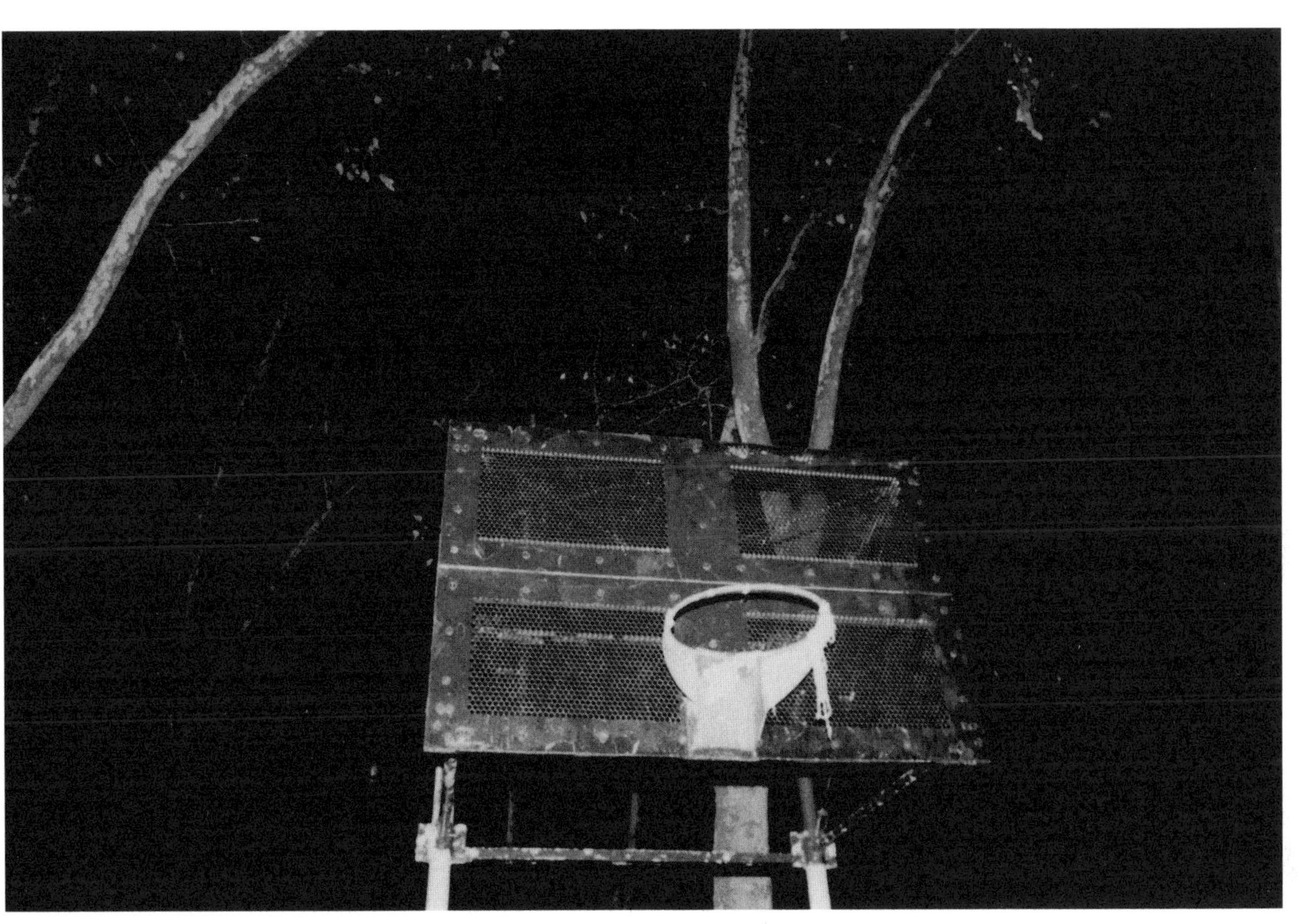

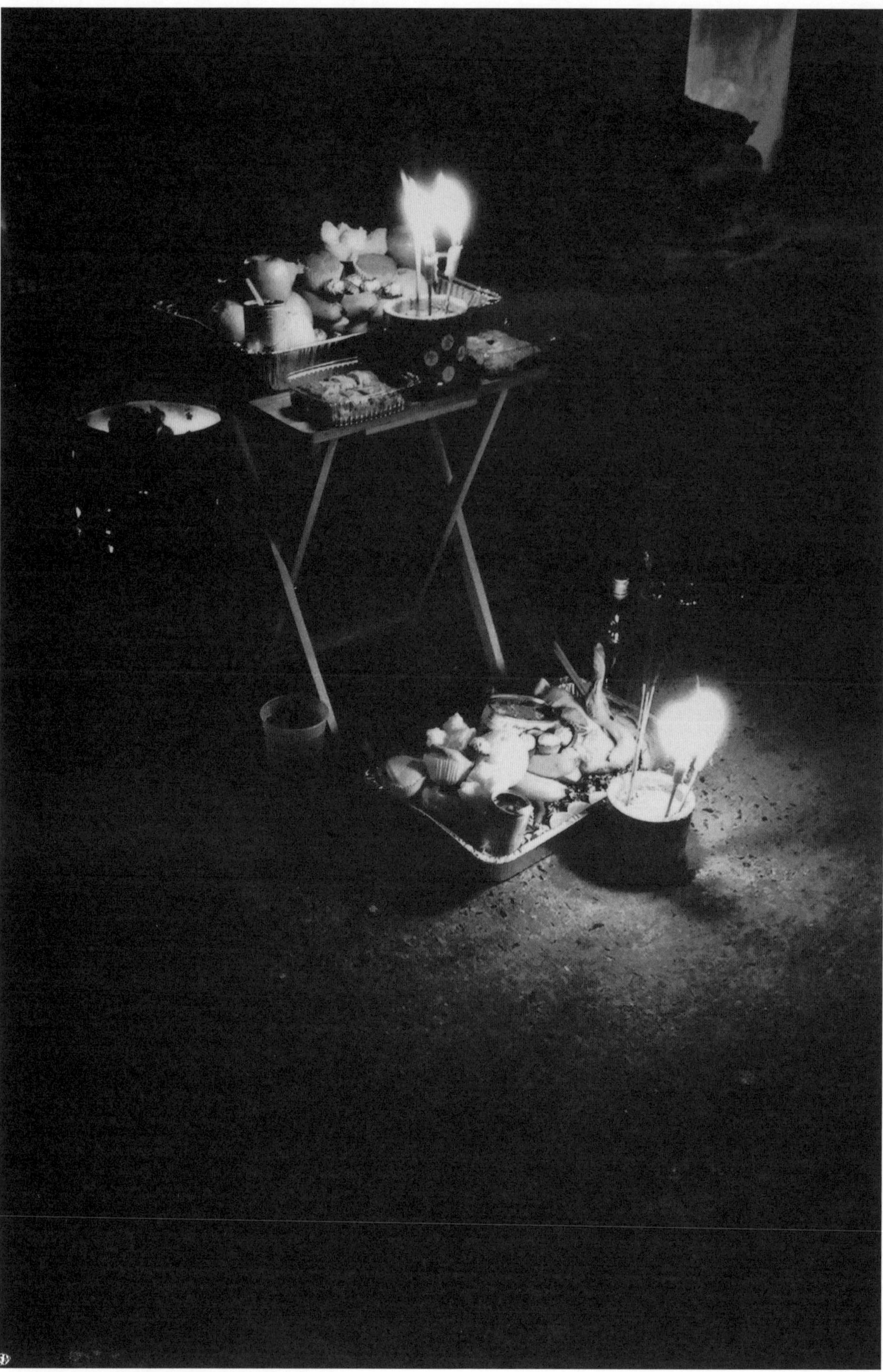

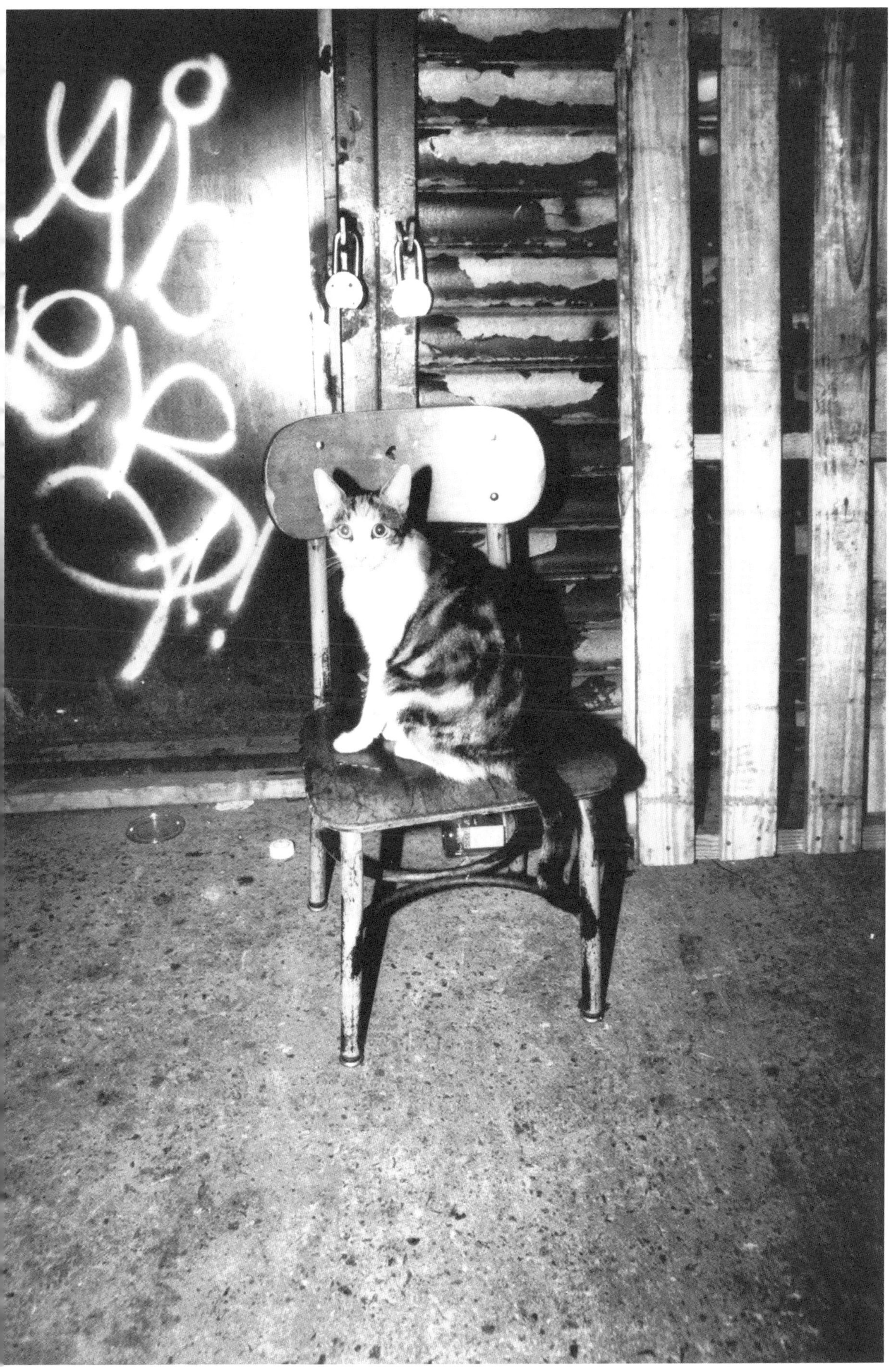

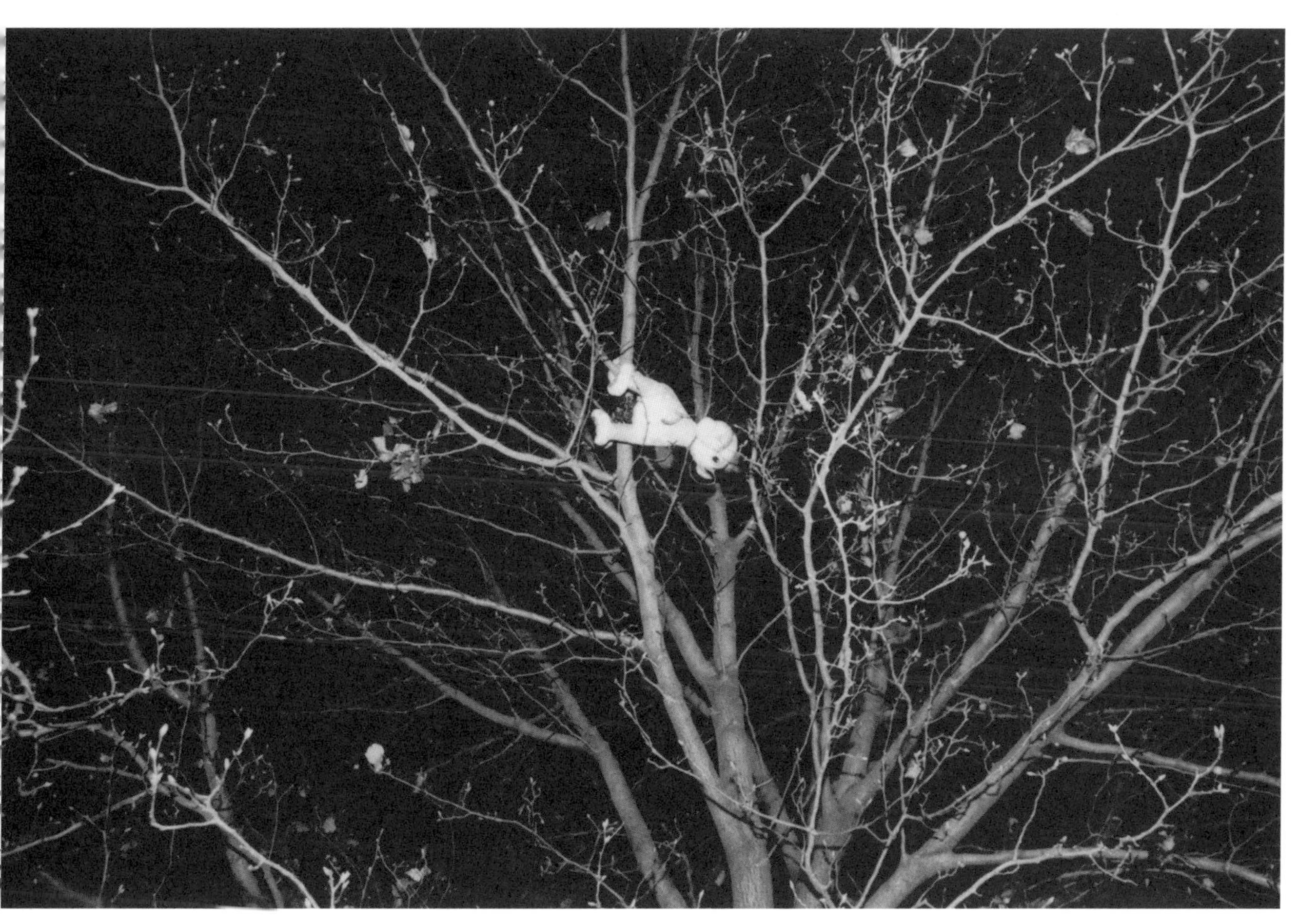

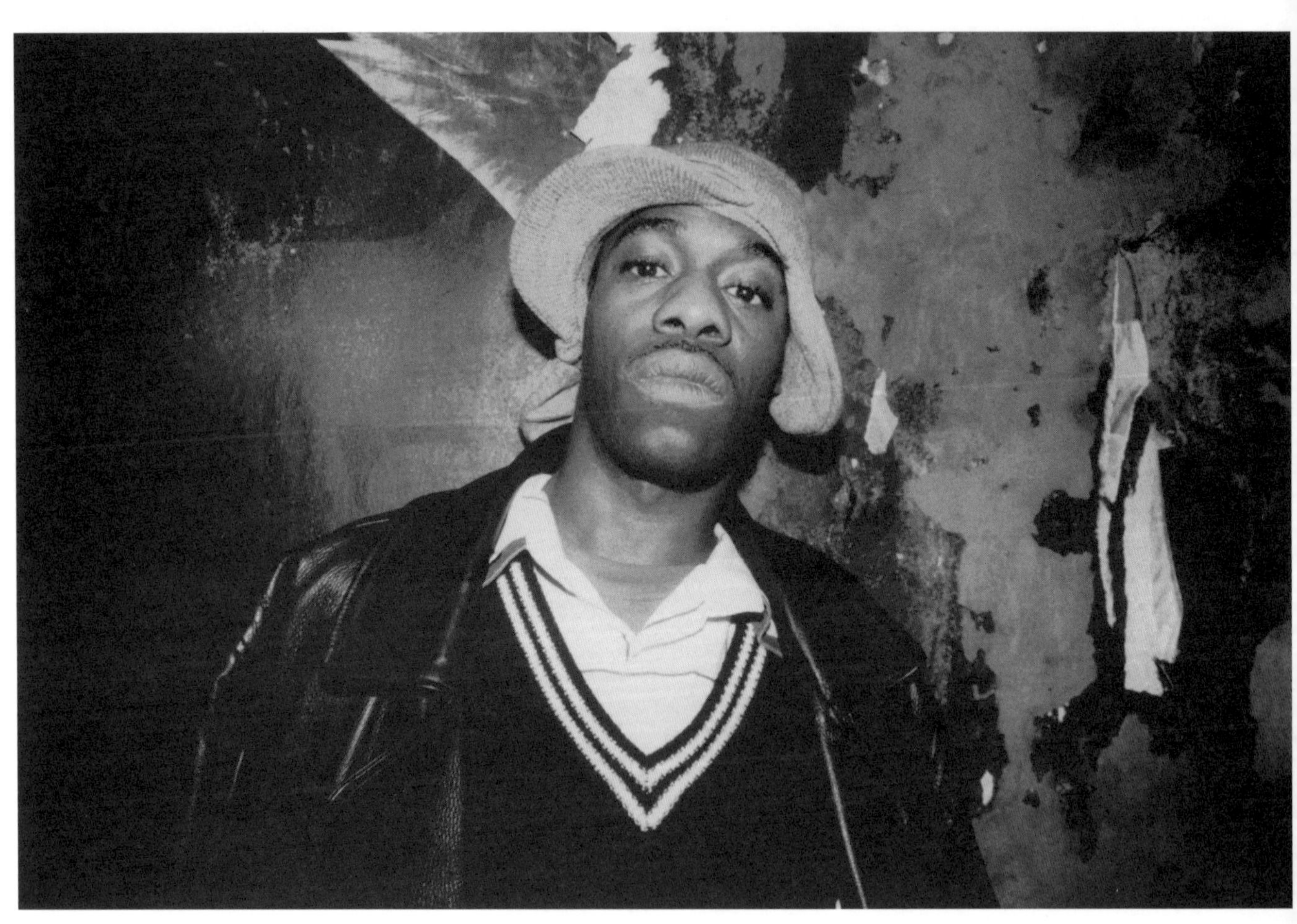

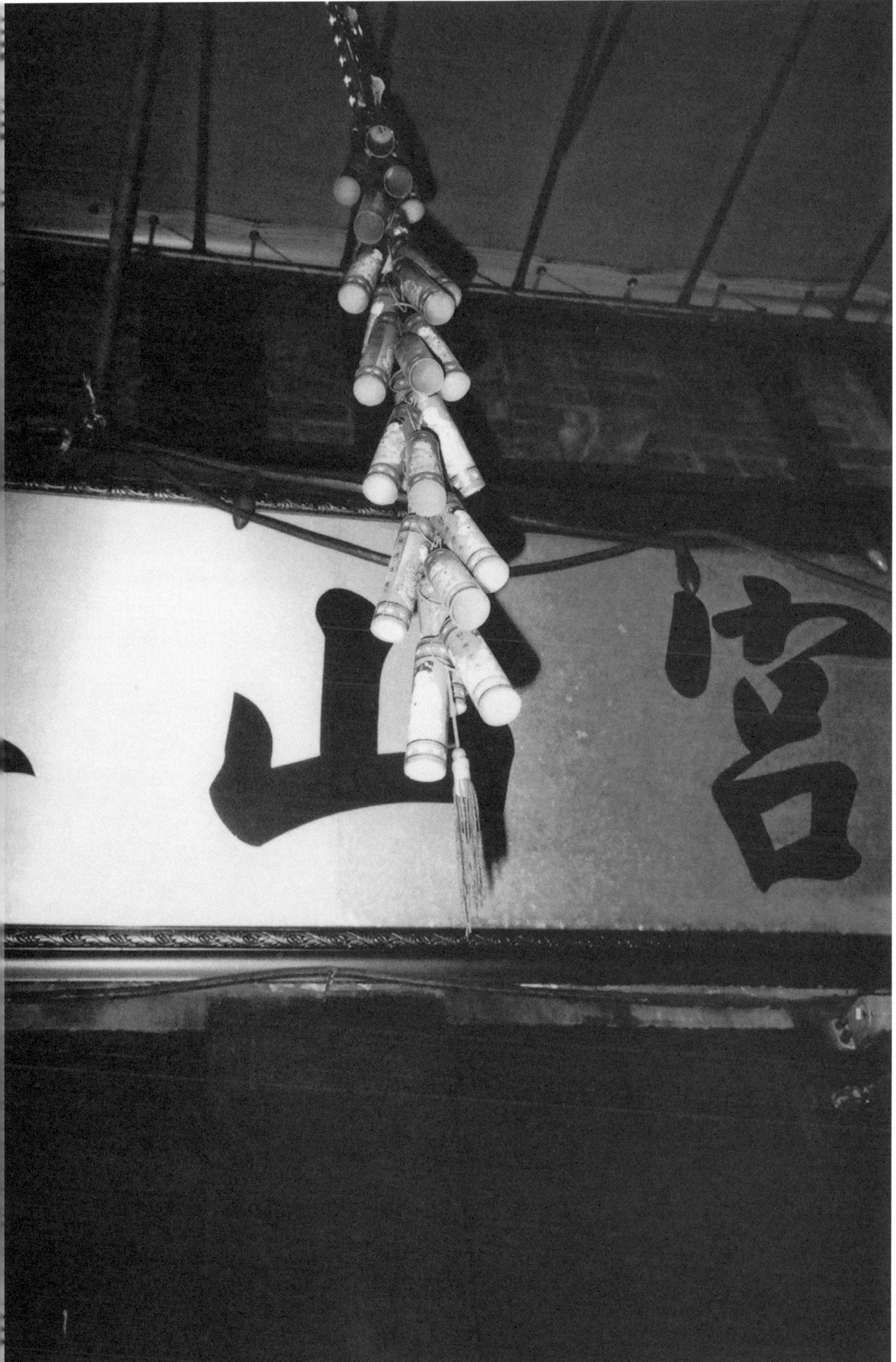

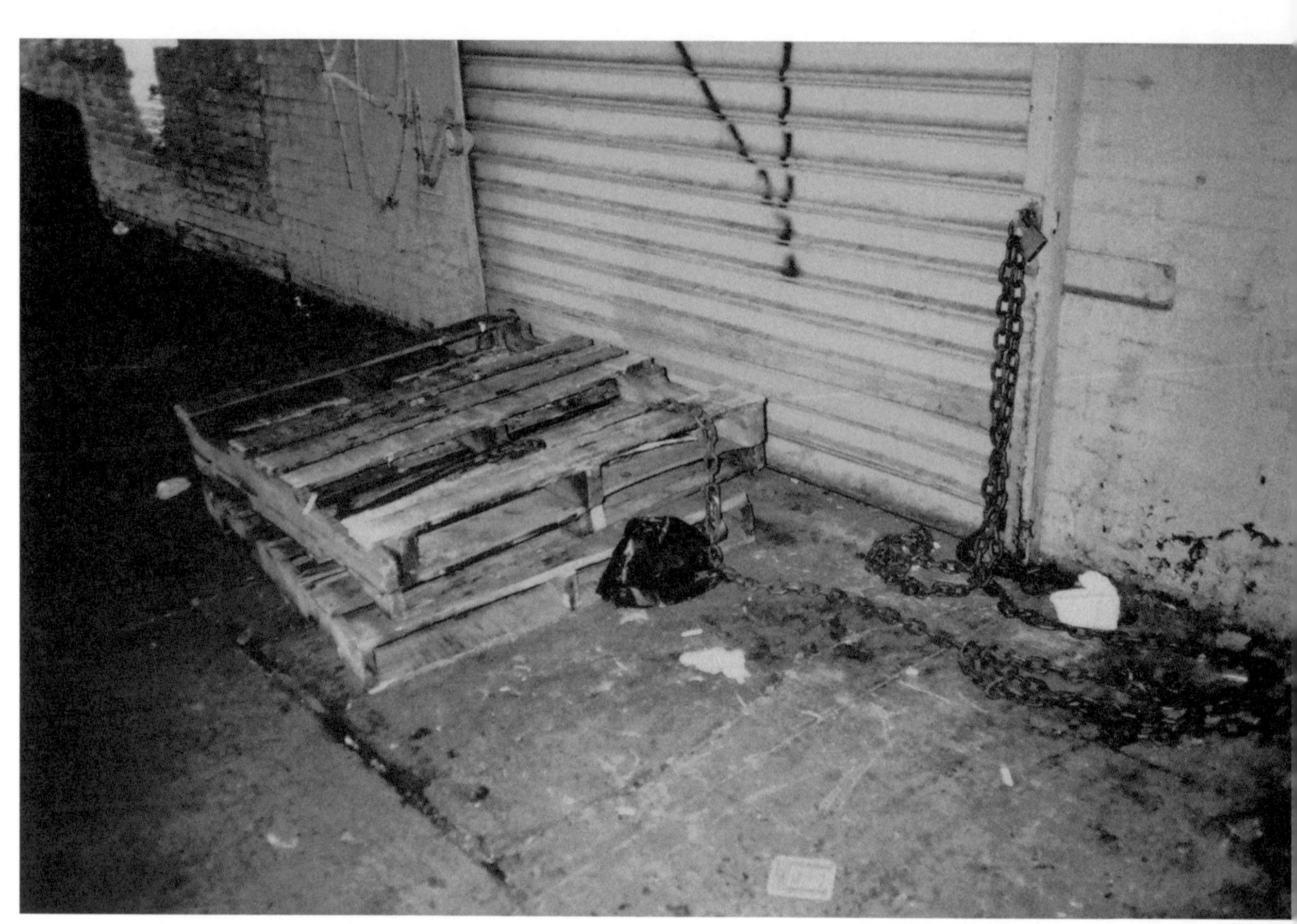

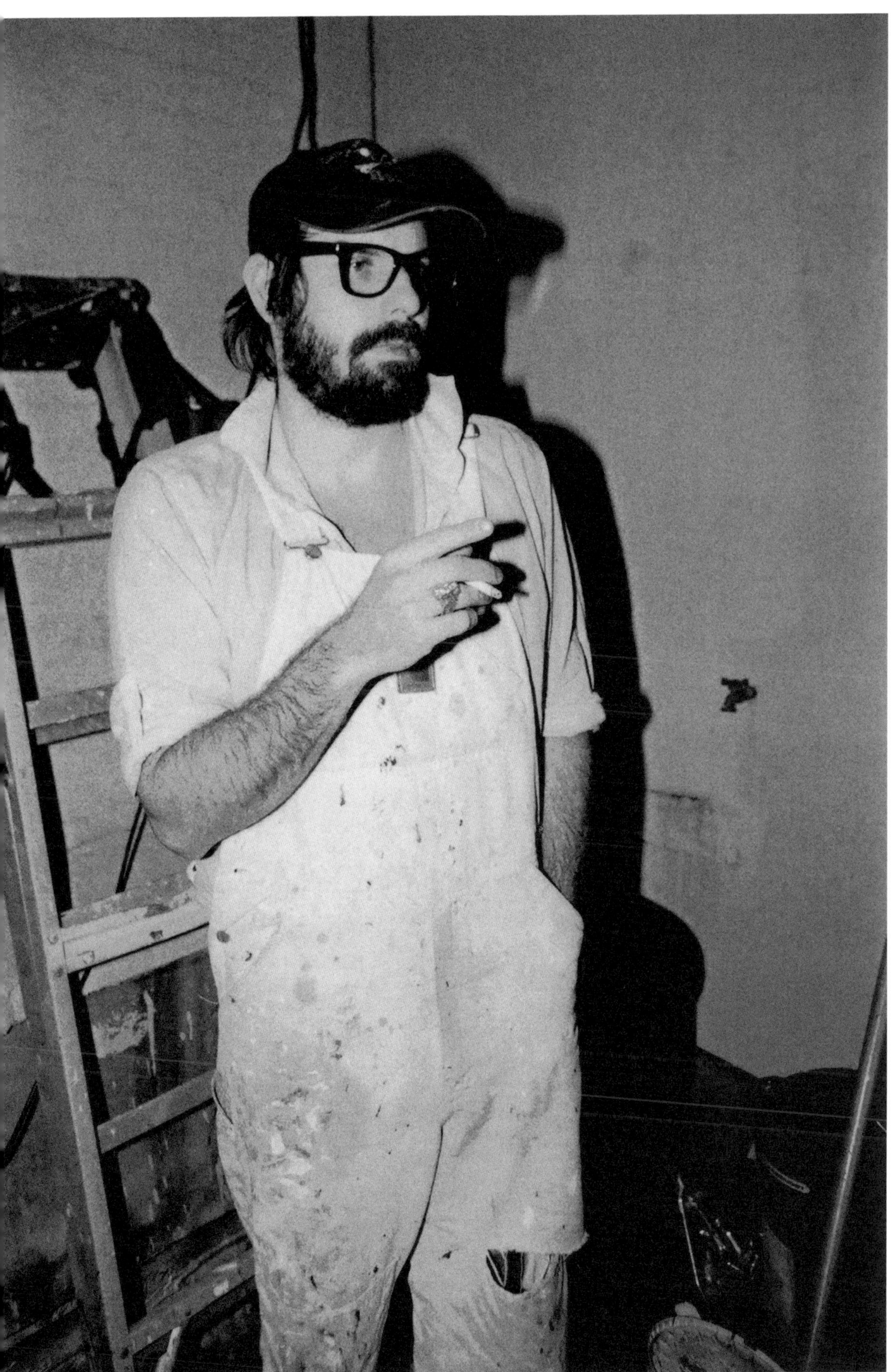

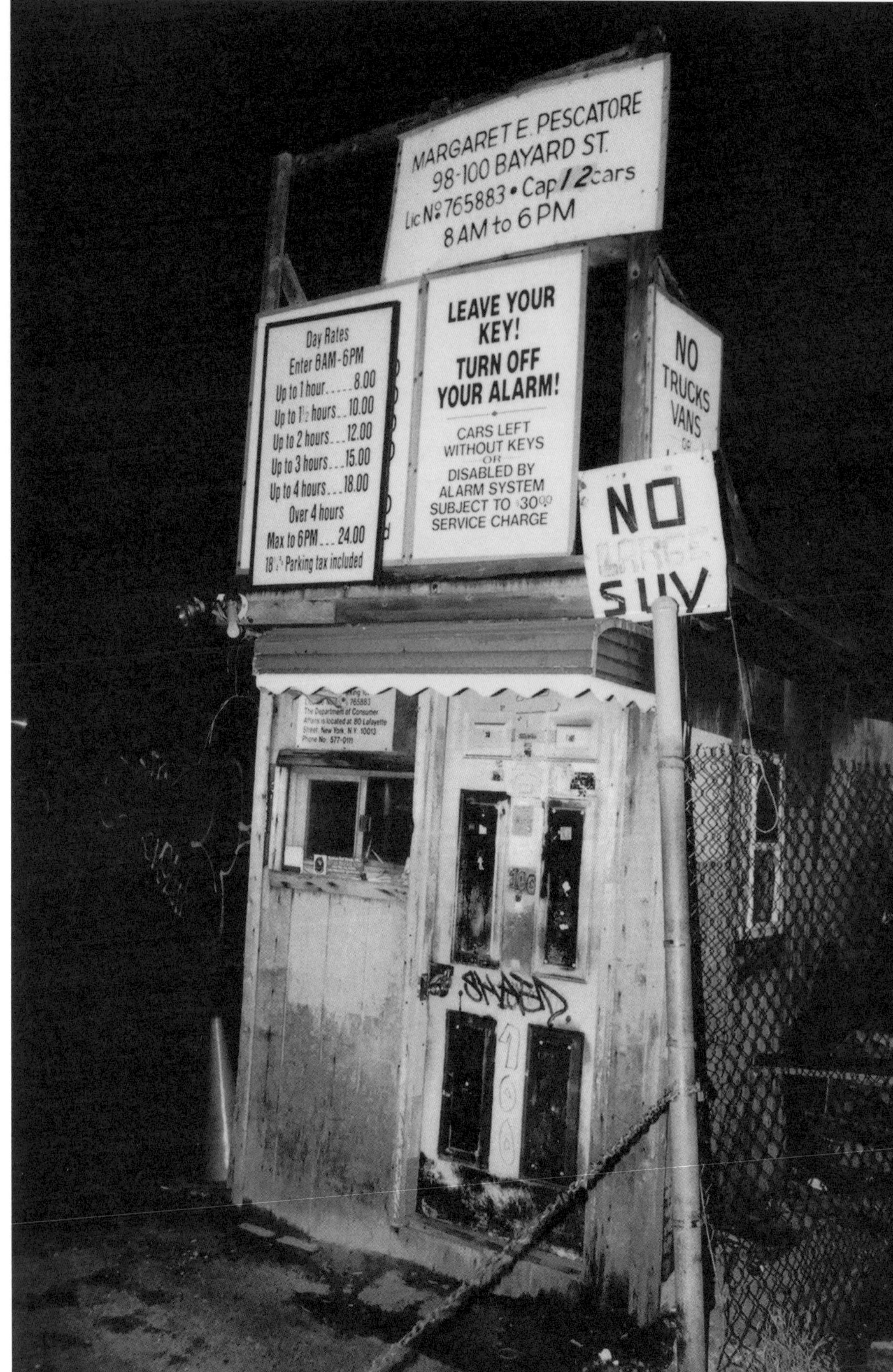
MARGARET E. PESCATORE
98-100 BAYARD ST.
Lic No 765883 • Cap 12 cars
8 AM to 6 PM
Day Rates
Enter 8AM-6PM
Up to 1 hour 8.00
Up to 1½ hours ... 10.00
Up to 2 hours ... 12.00
Up to 3 hours ... 15.00
Up to 4 hours ... 18.00
Over 4 hours
Max to 6PM ... 24.00
Parking tax included
LEAVE YOUR KEY!
TURN OFF YOUR ALARM!
CARS LEFT WITHOUT KEYS OR DISABLED BY ALARM SYSTEM SUBJECT TO $30.00 SERVICE CHARGE
NO TRUCKS VANS
NO
SUV

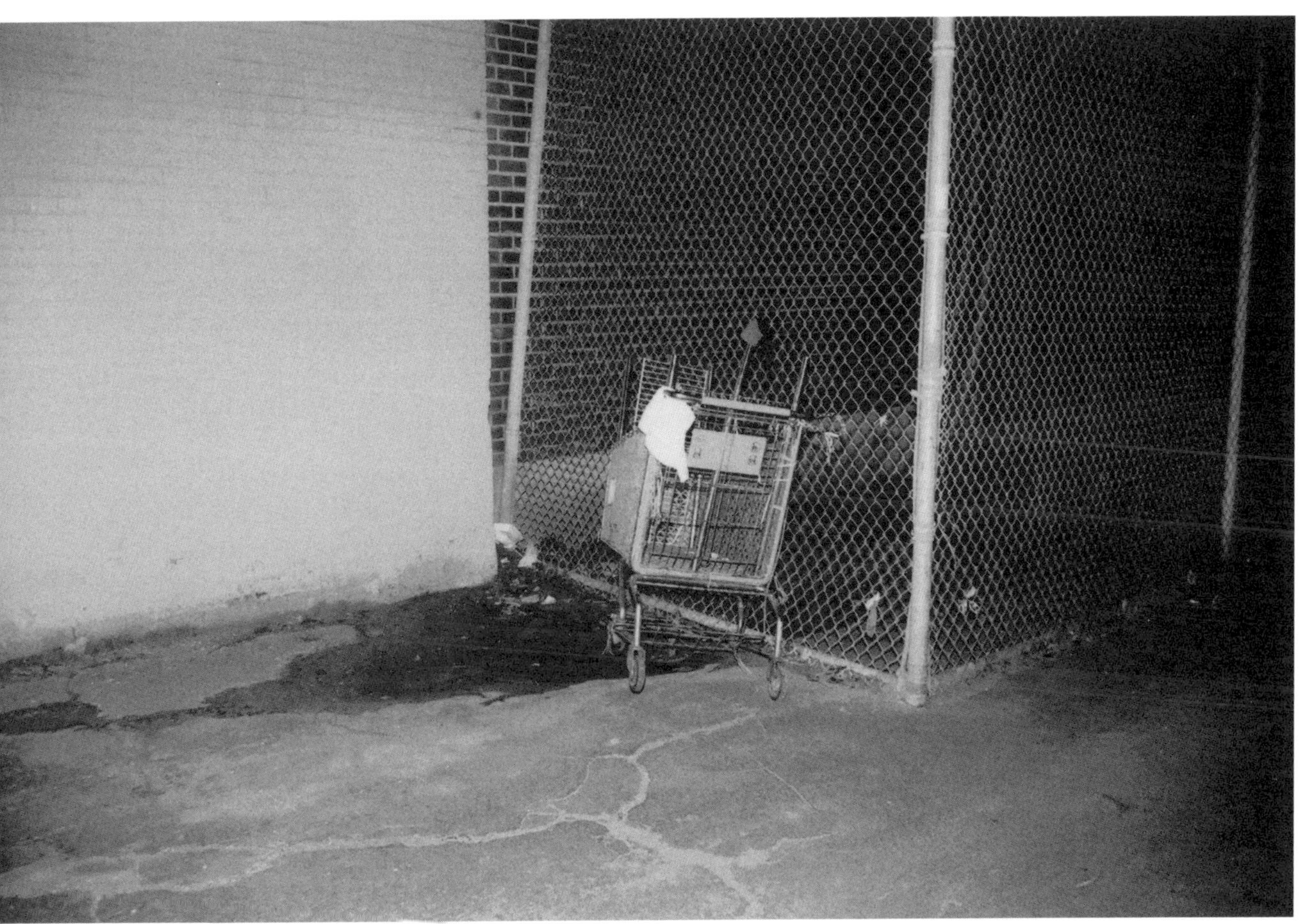

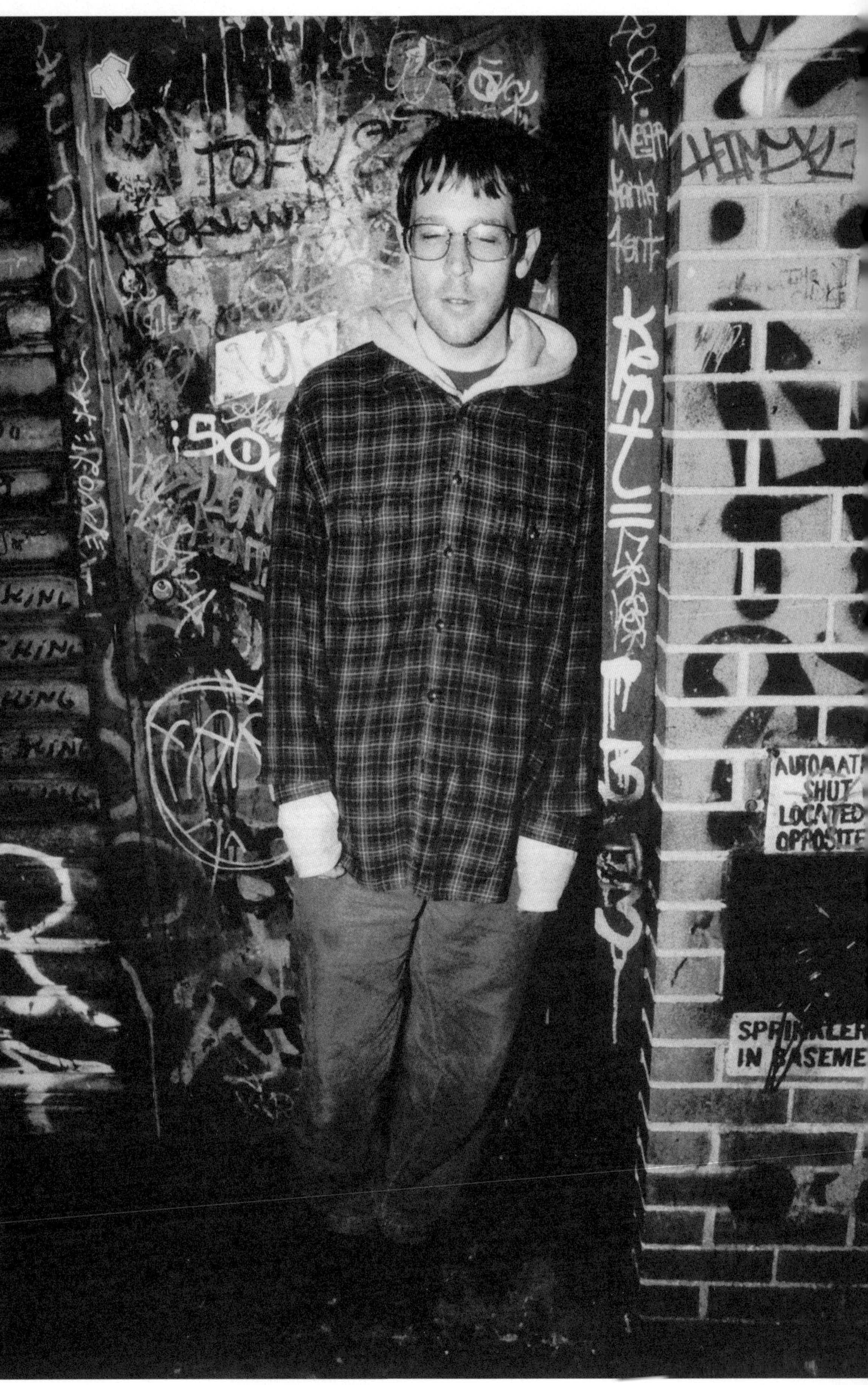
AUTOMAT
SHUT
LOCATED
OPPOSITE
SPRINKLER
IN BASEME

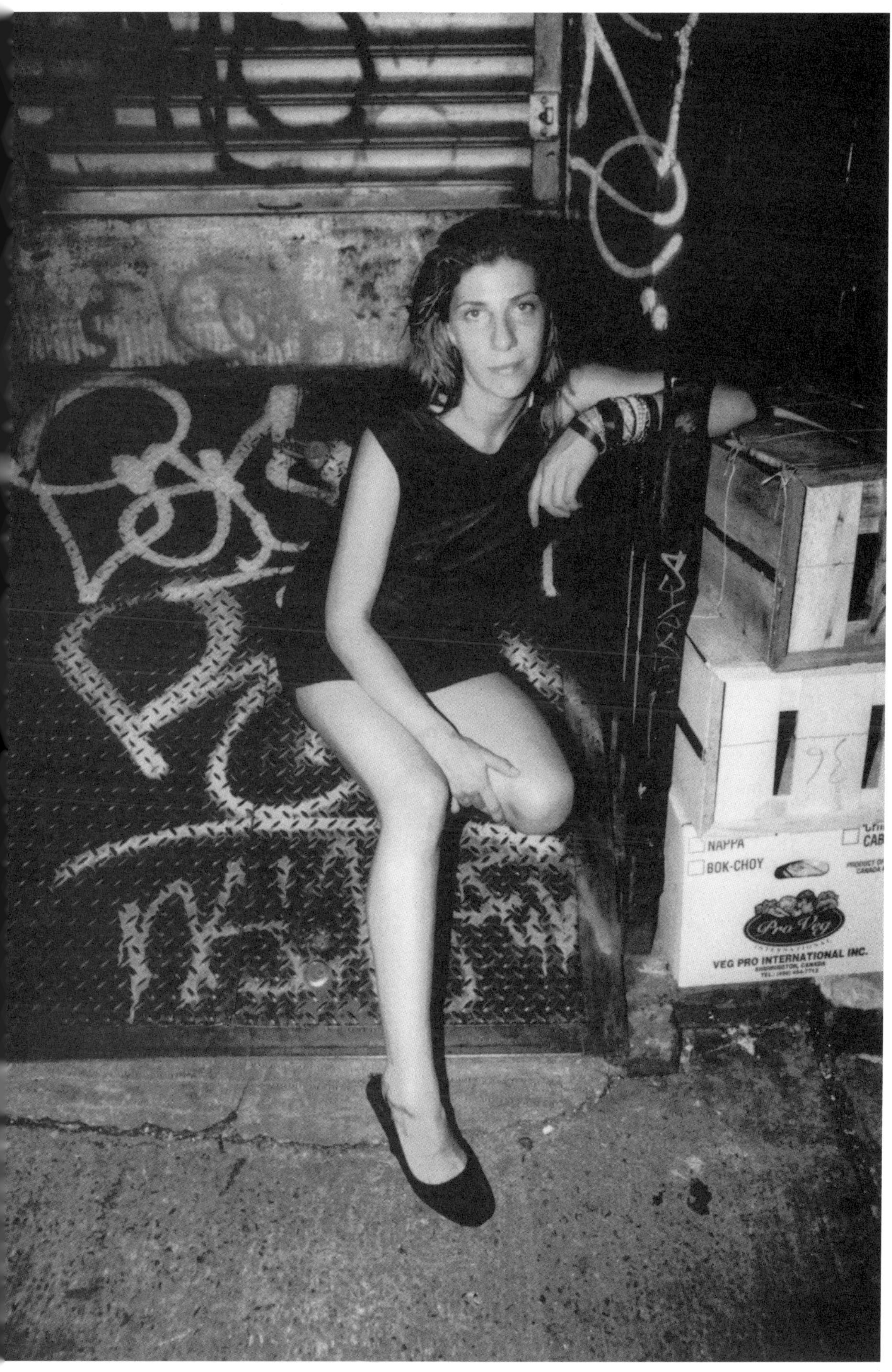
NAPPA
BOK-CHOY
Pro-Veg
VEG PRO INTERNATIONAL INC.

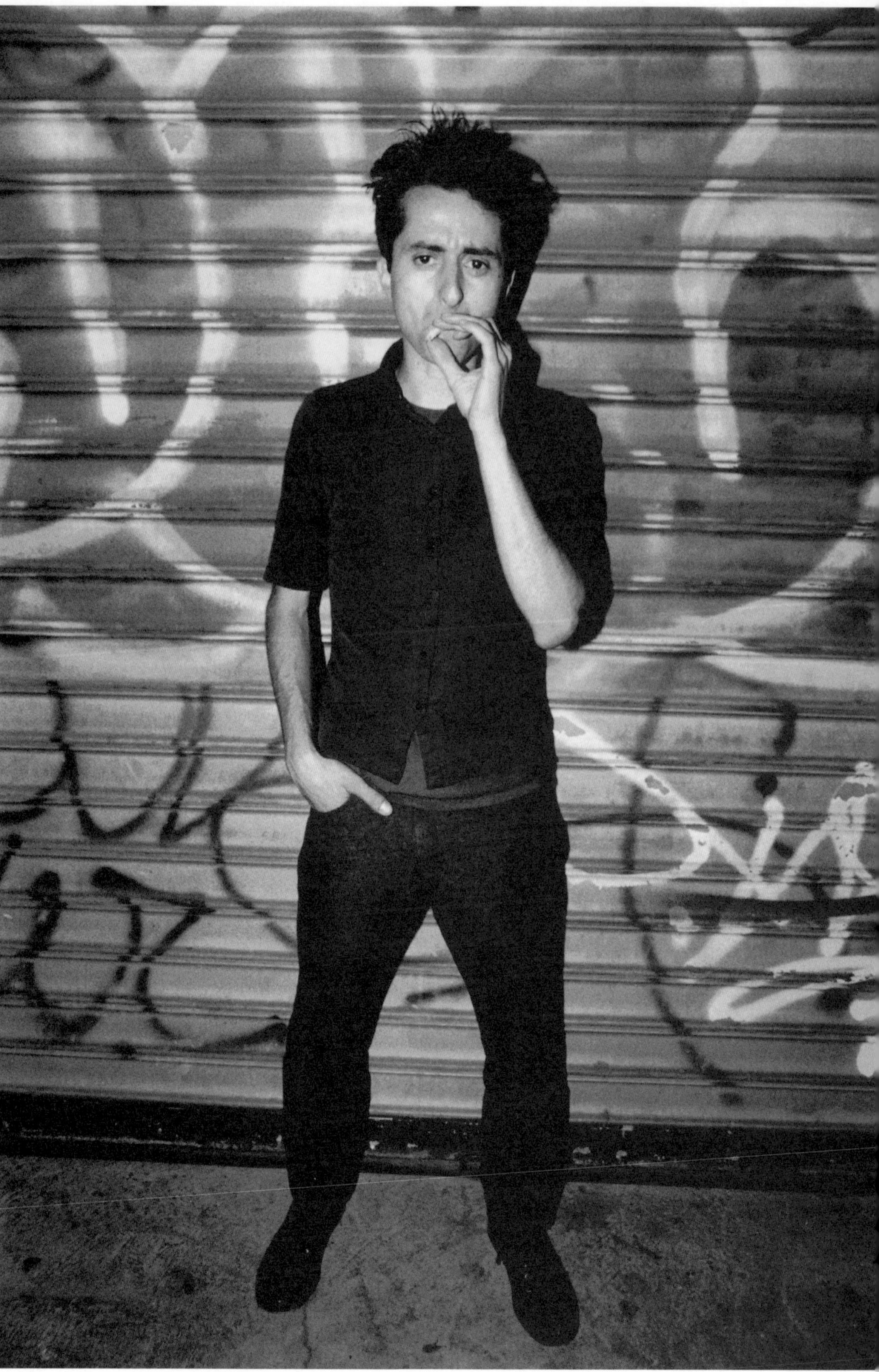

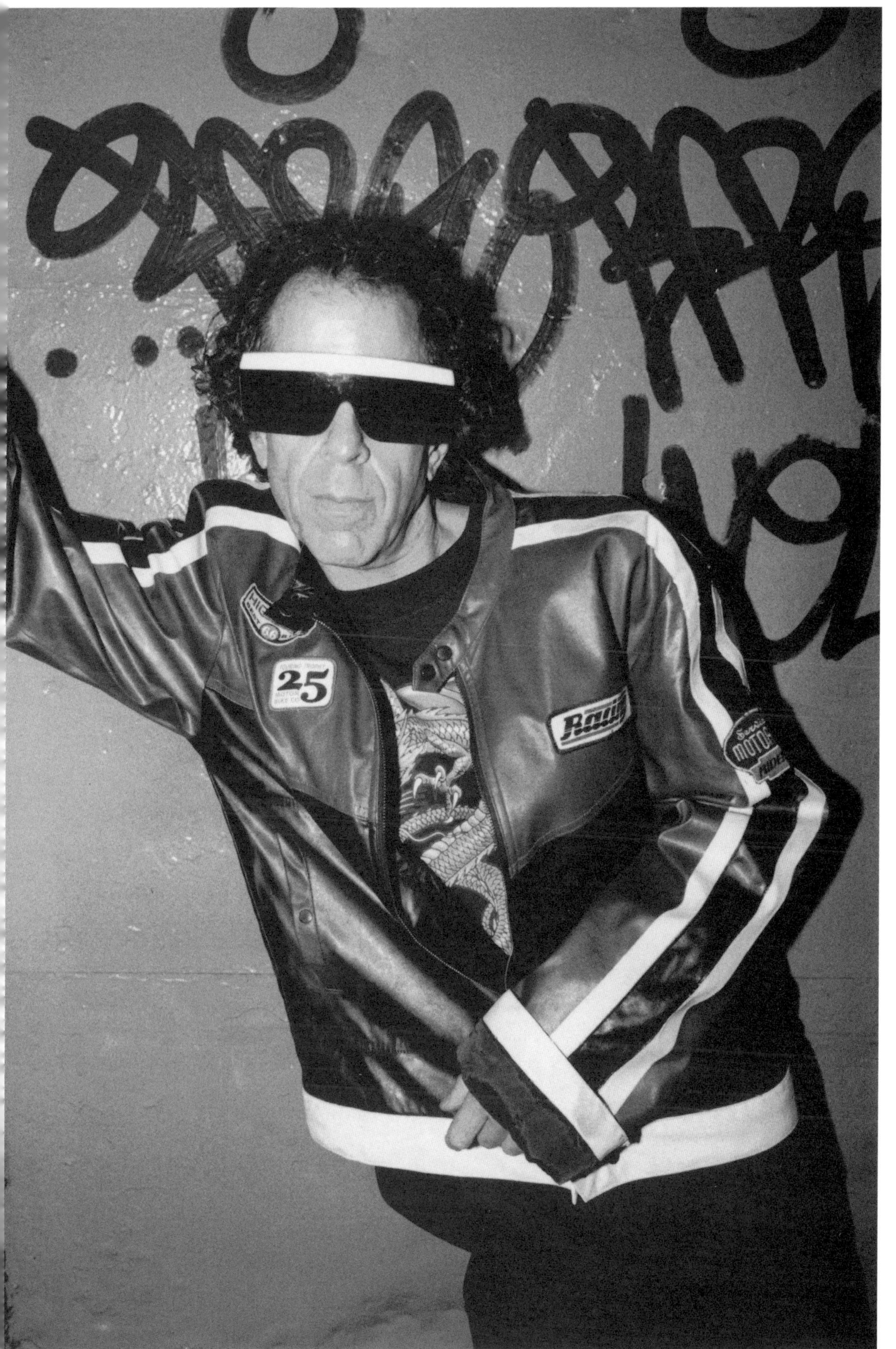
25

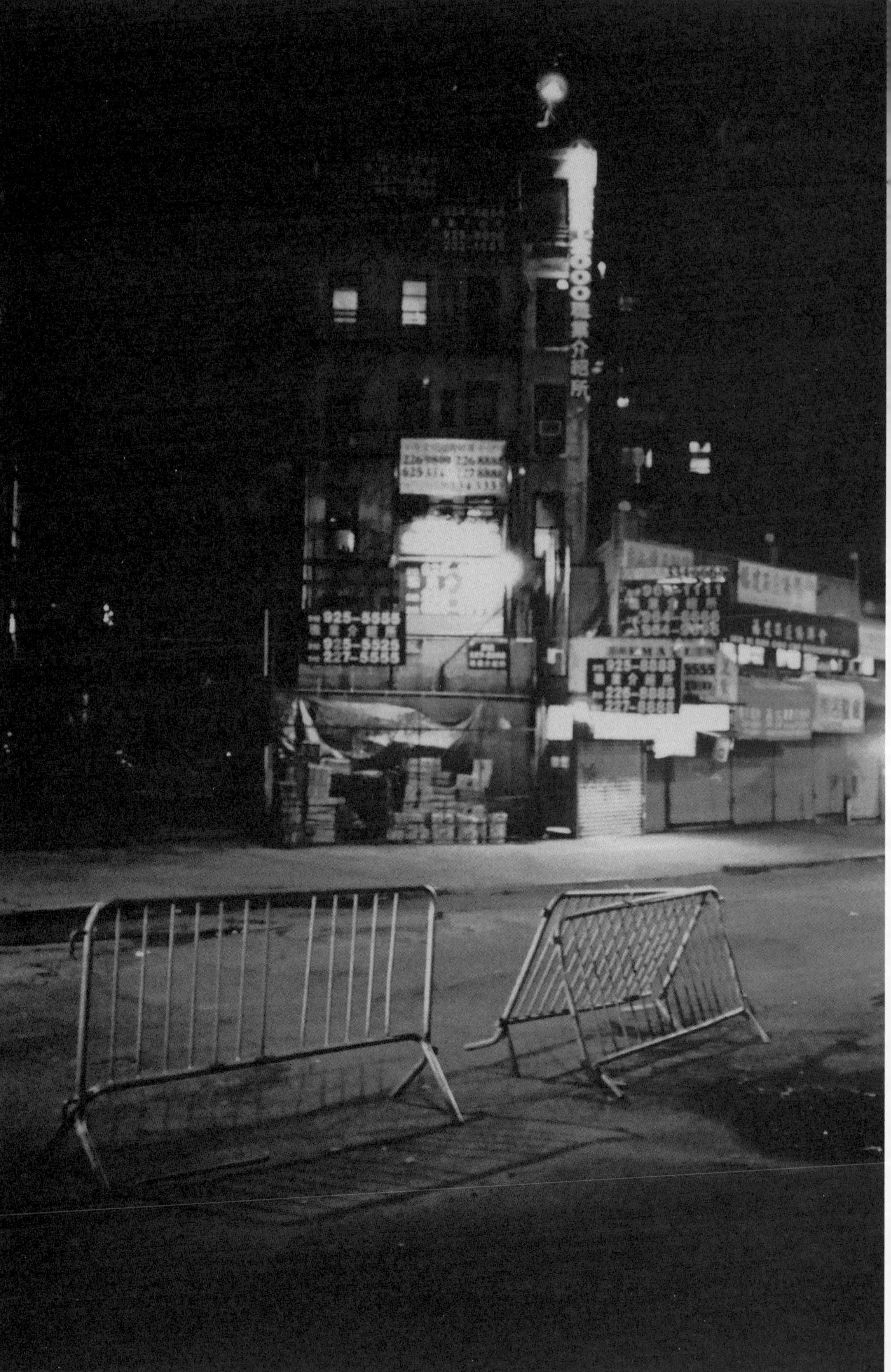
職業介紹所
925-5555
925-9929
227-5555

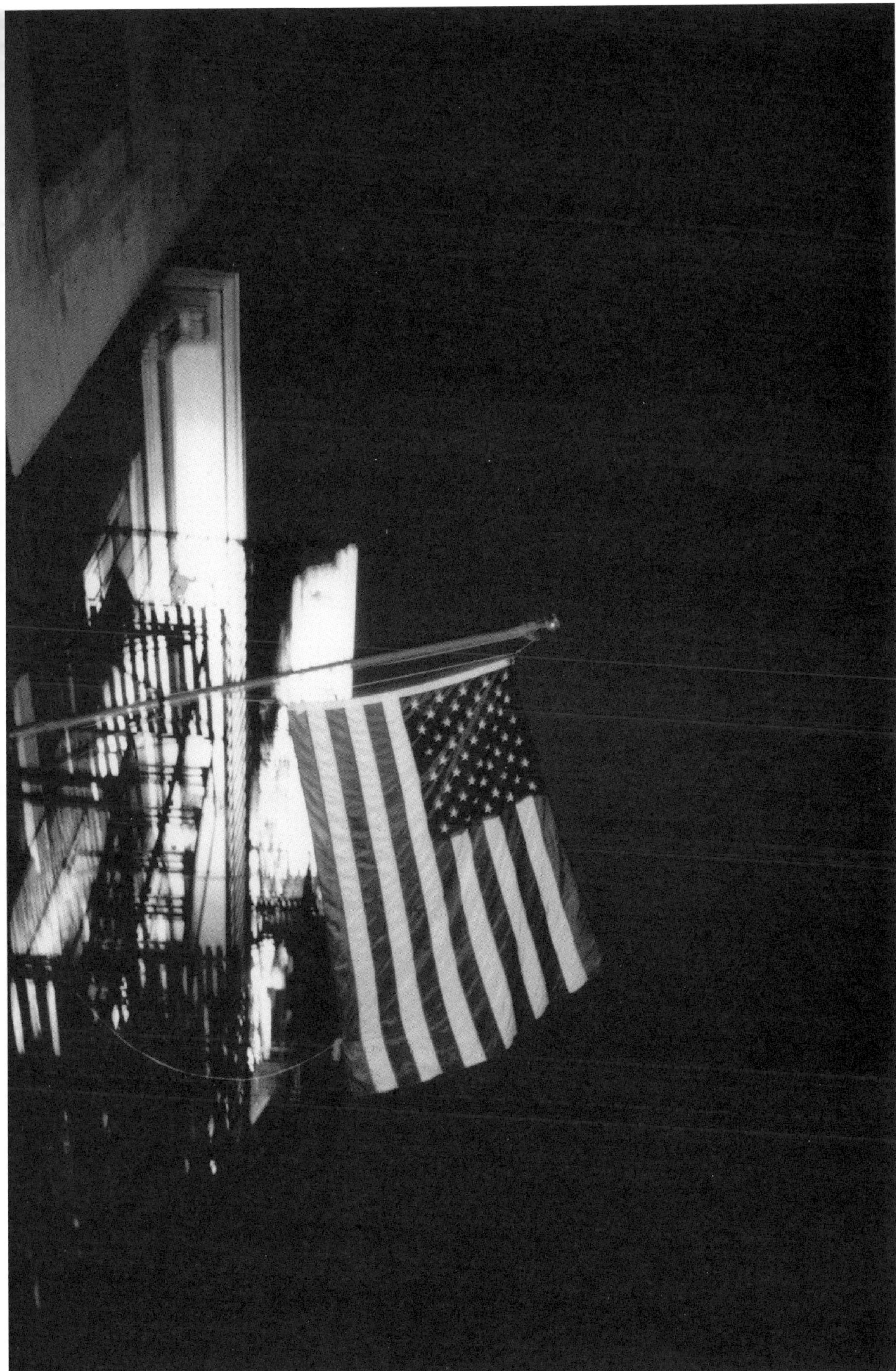

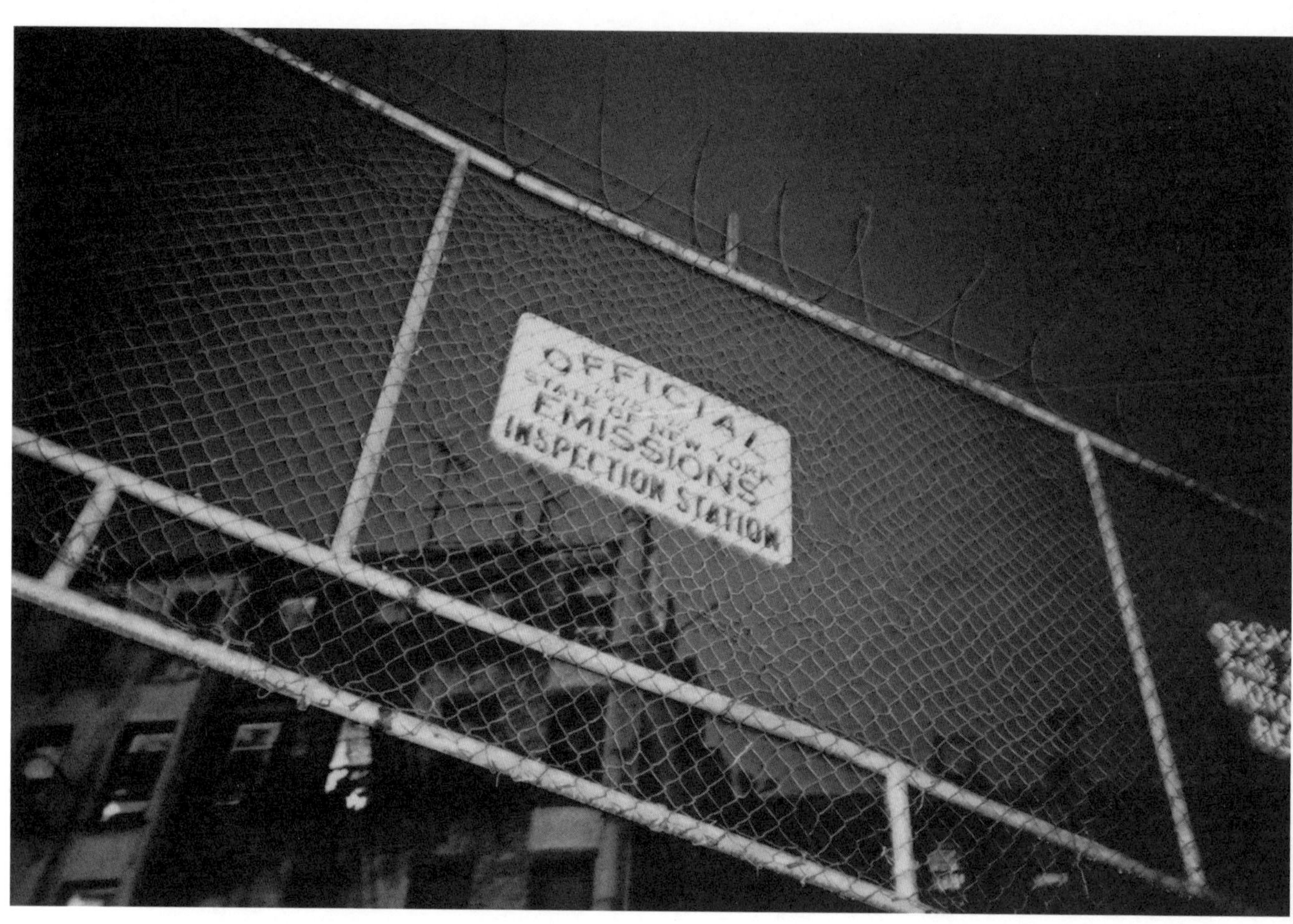
OFFICIAL
STATE OF NEW YORK
EMISSIONS
INSPECTION STATION

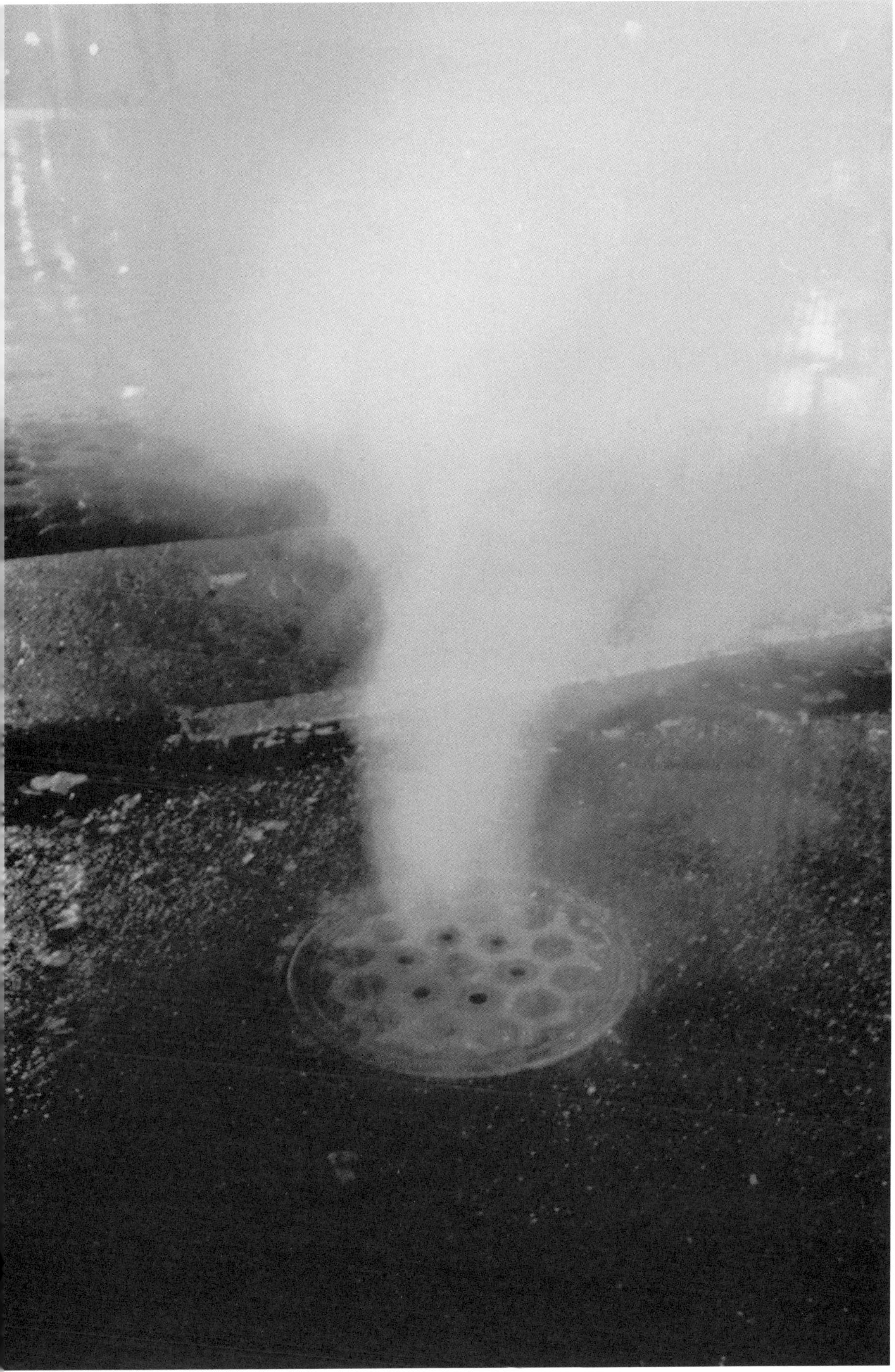

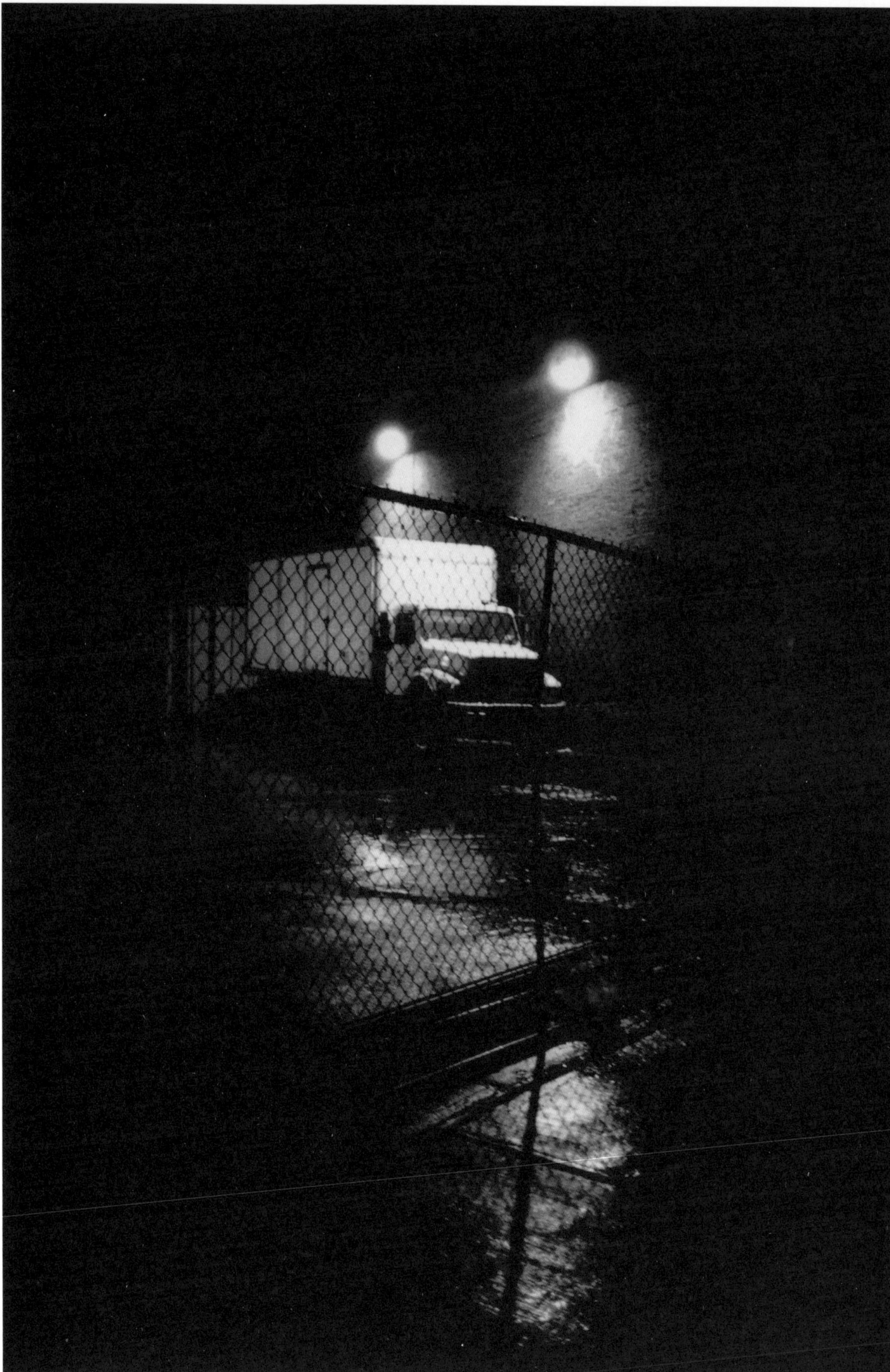

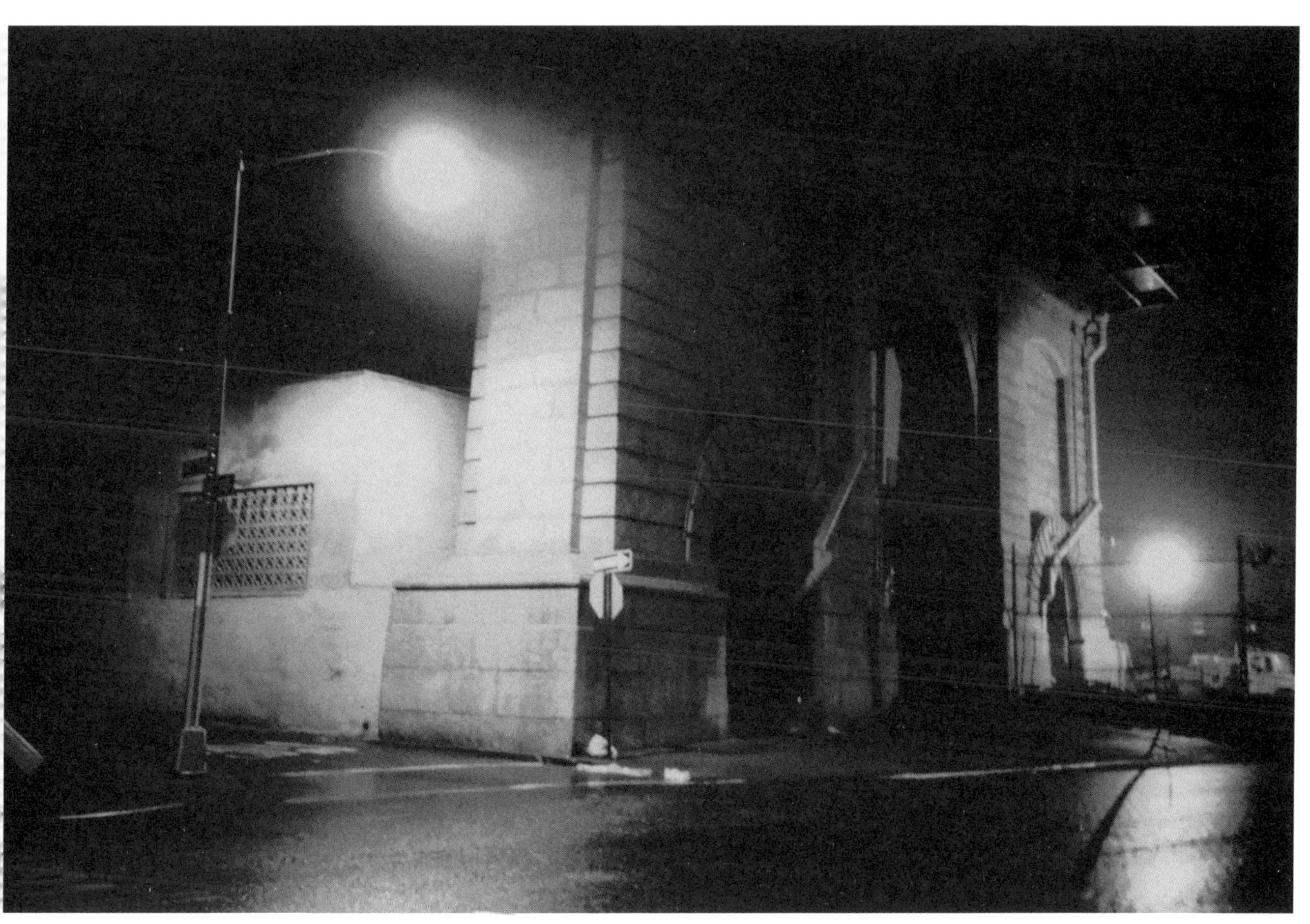

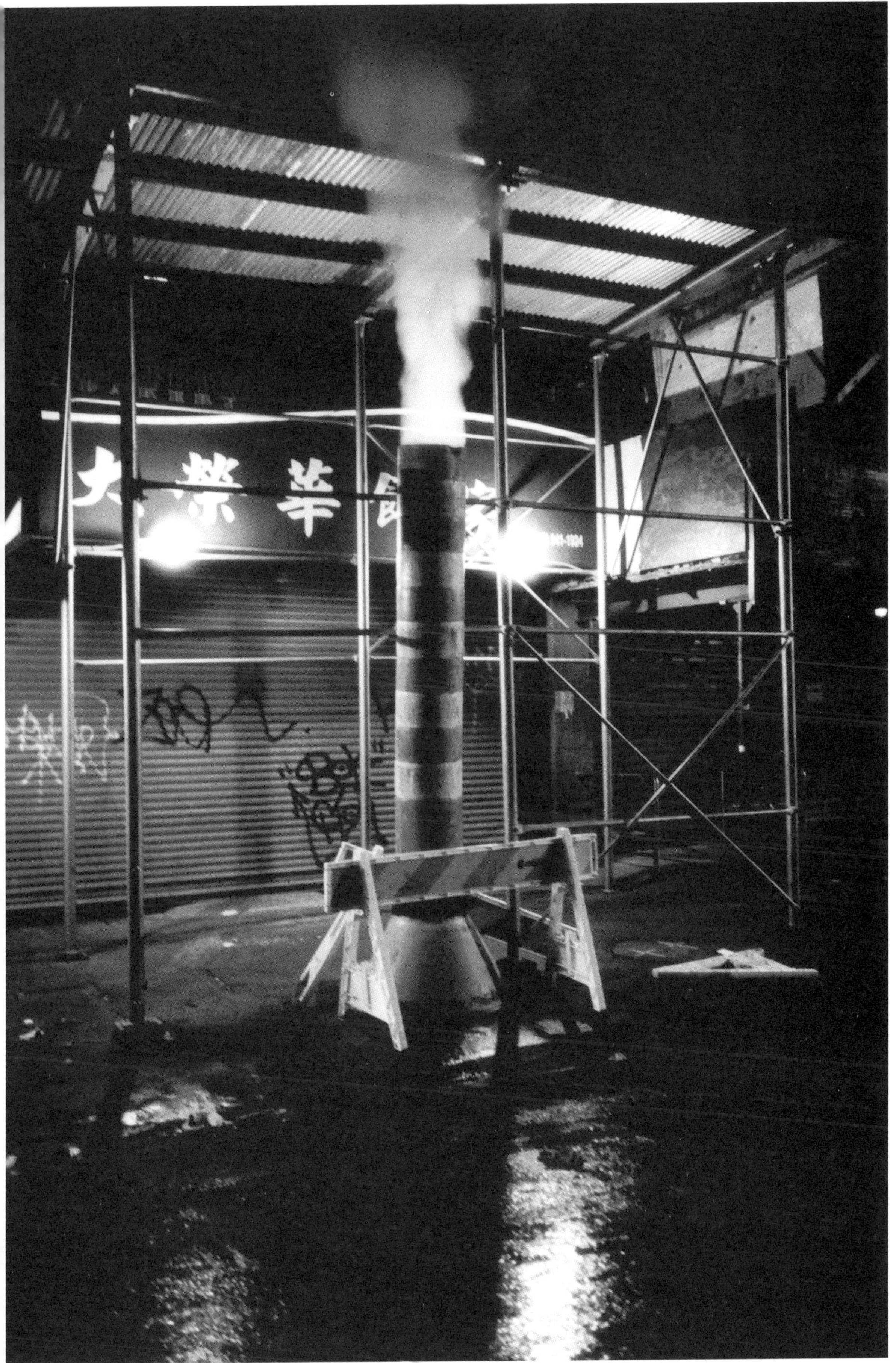

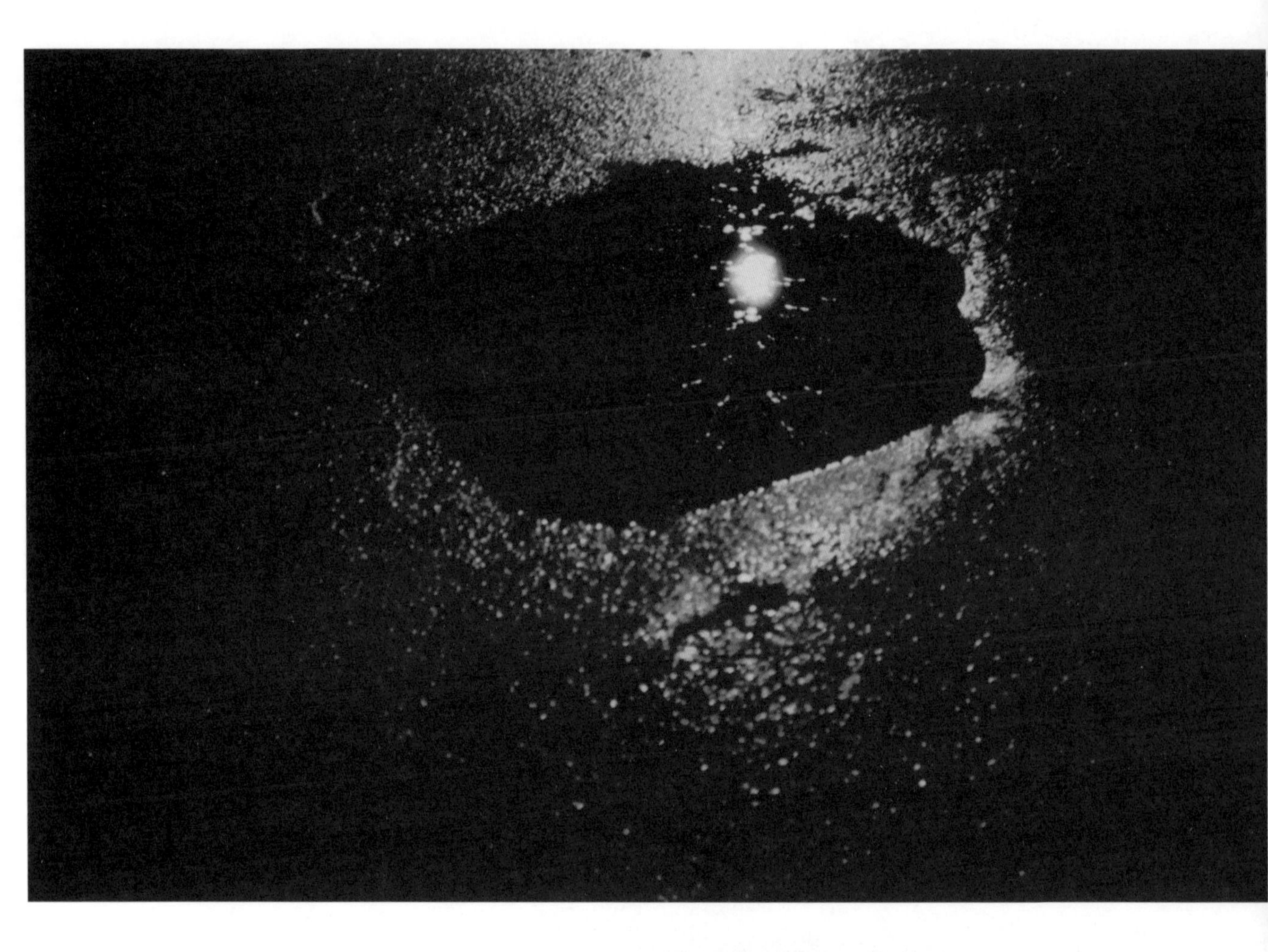

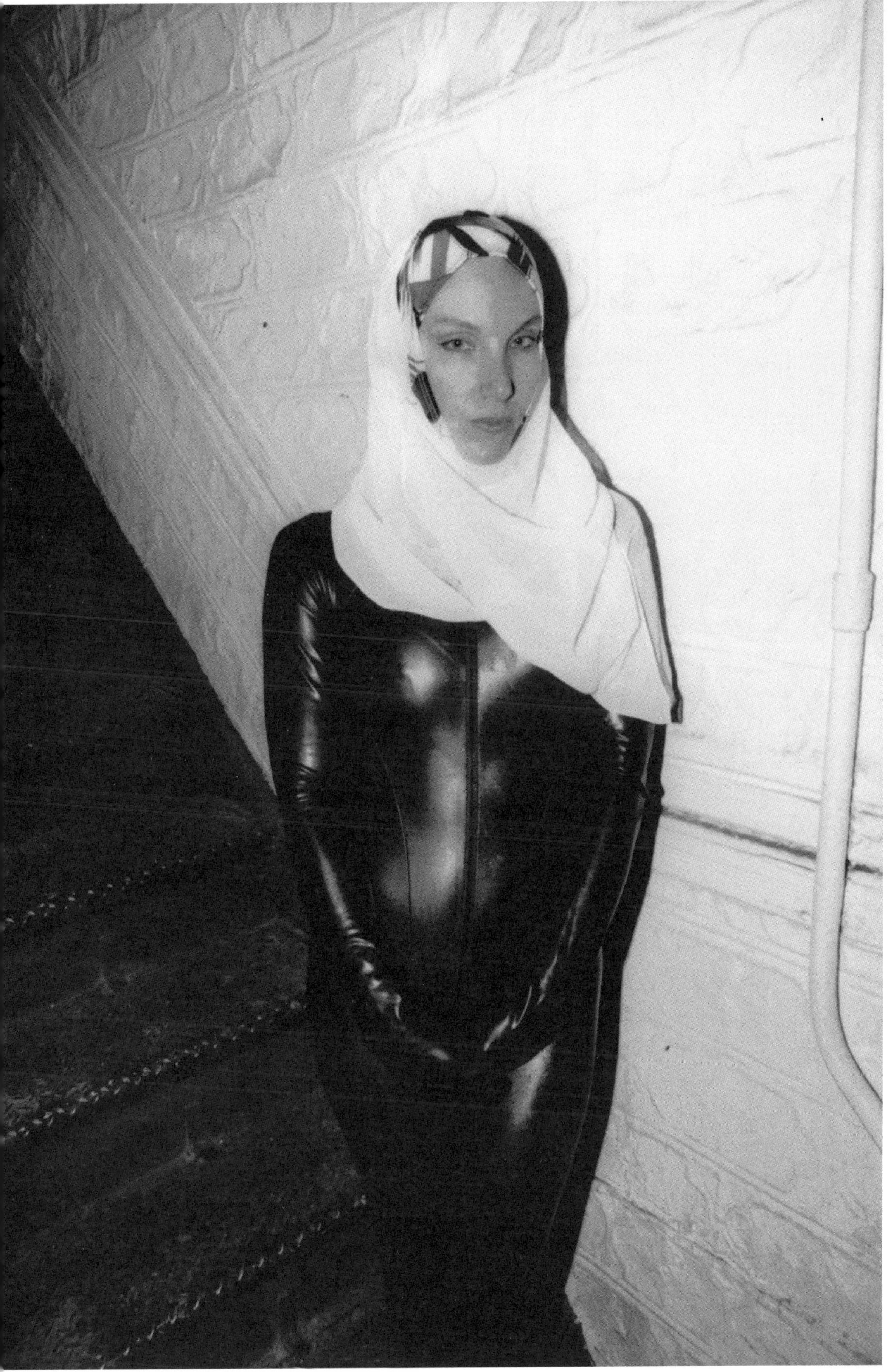

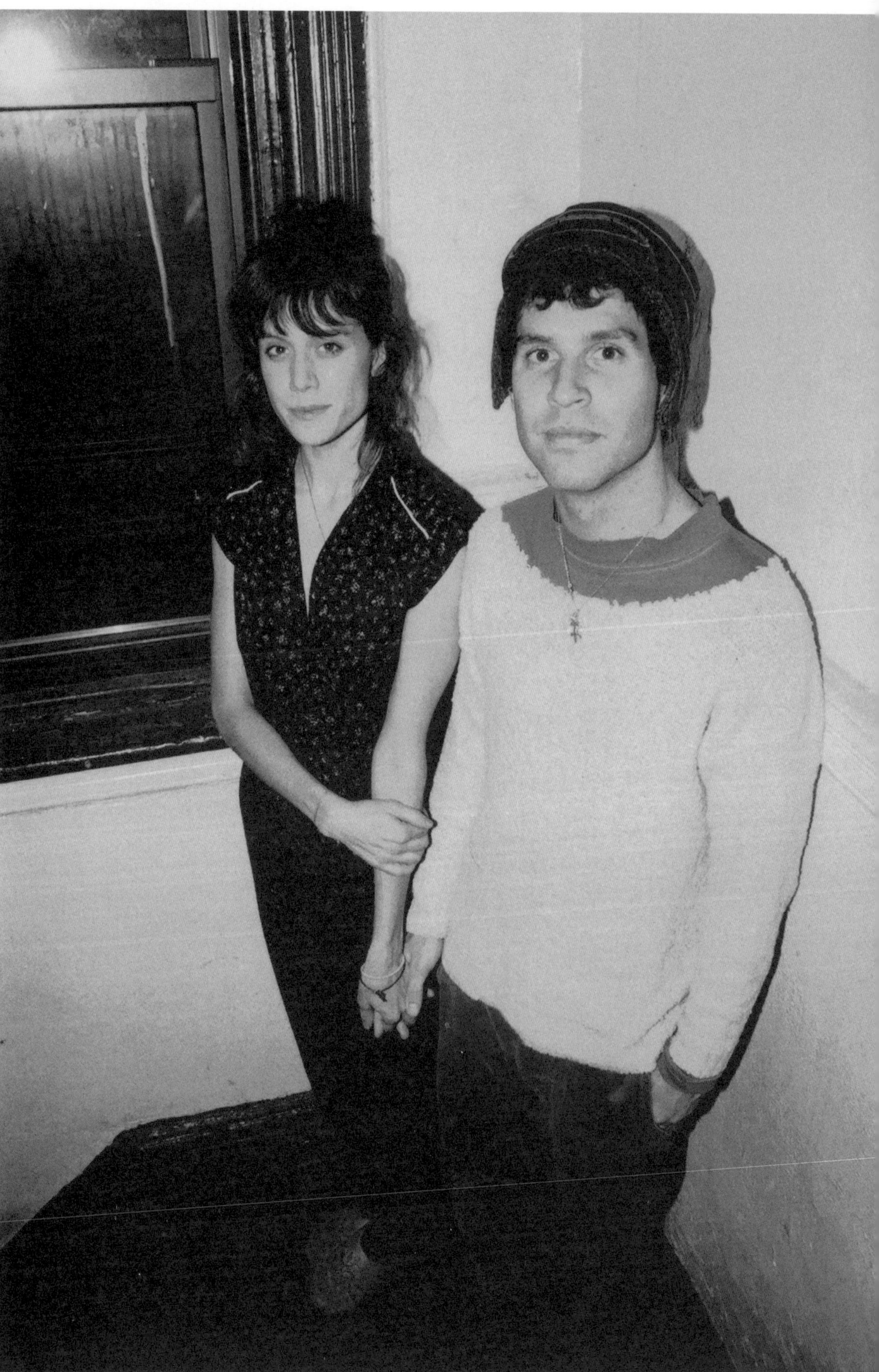

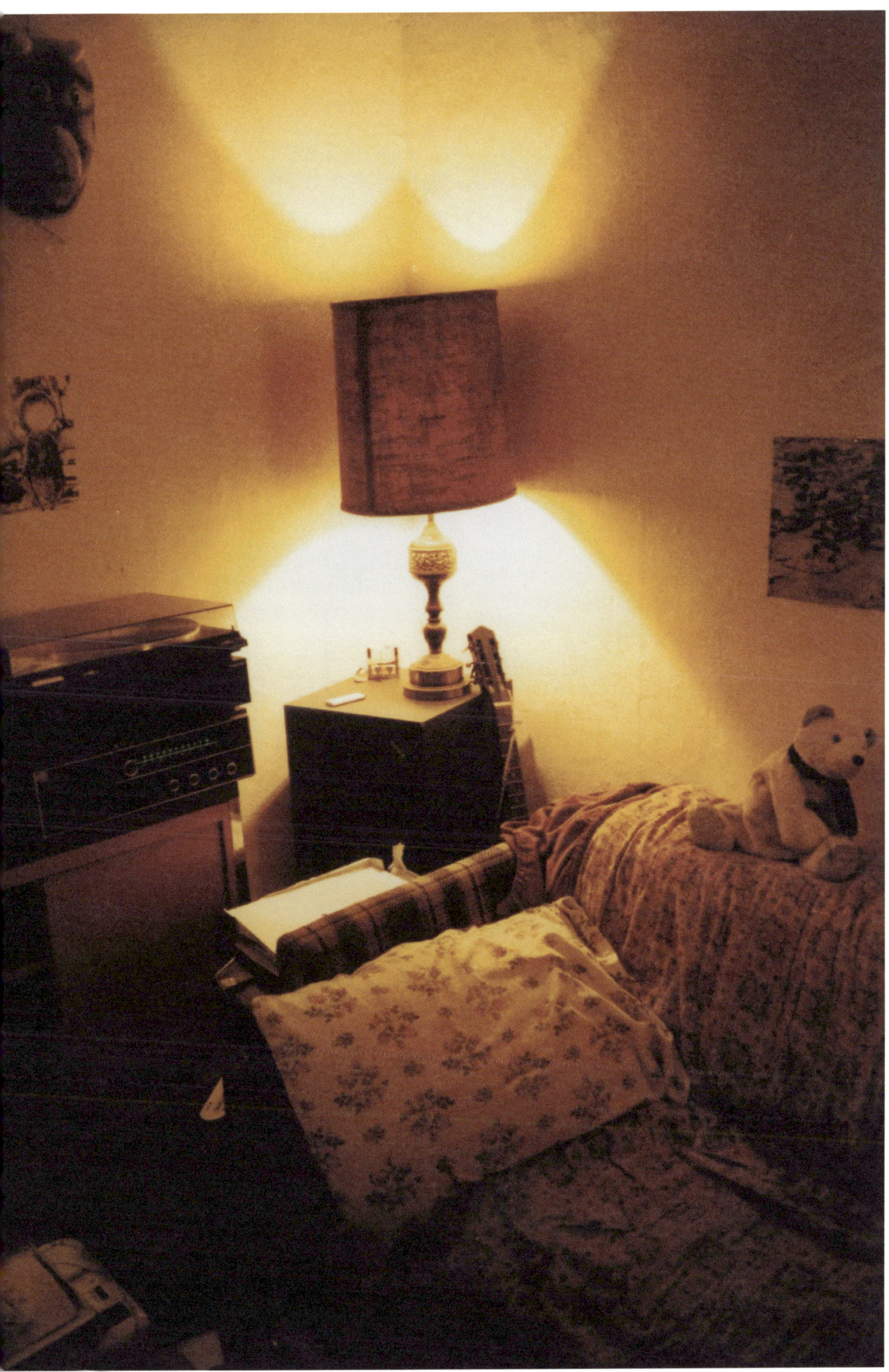

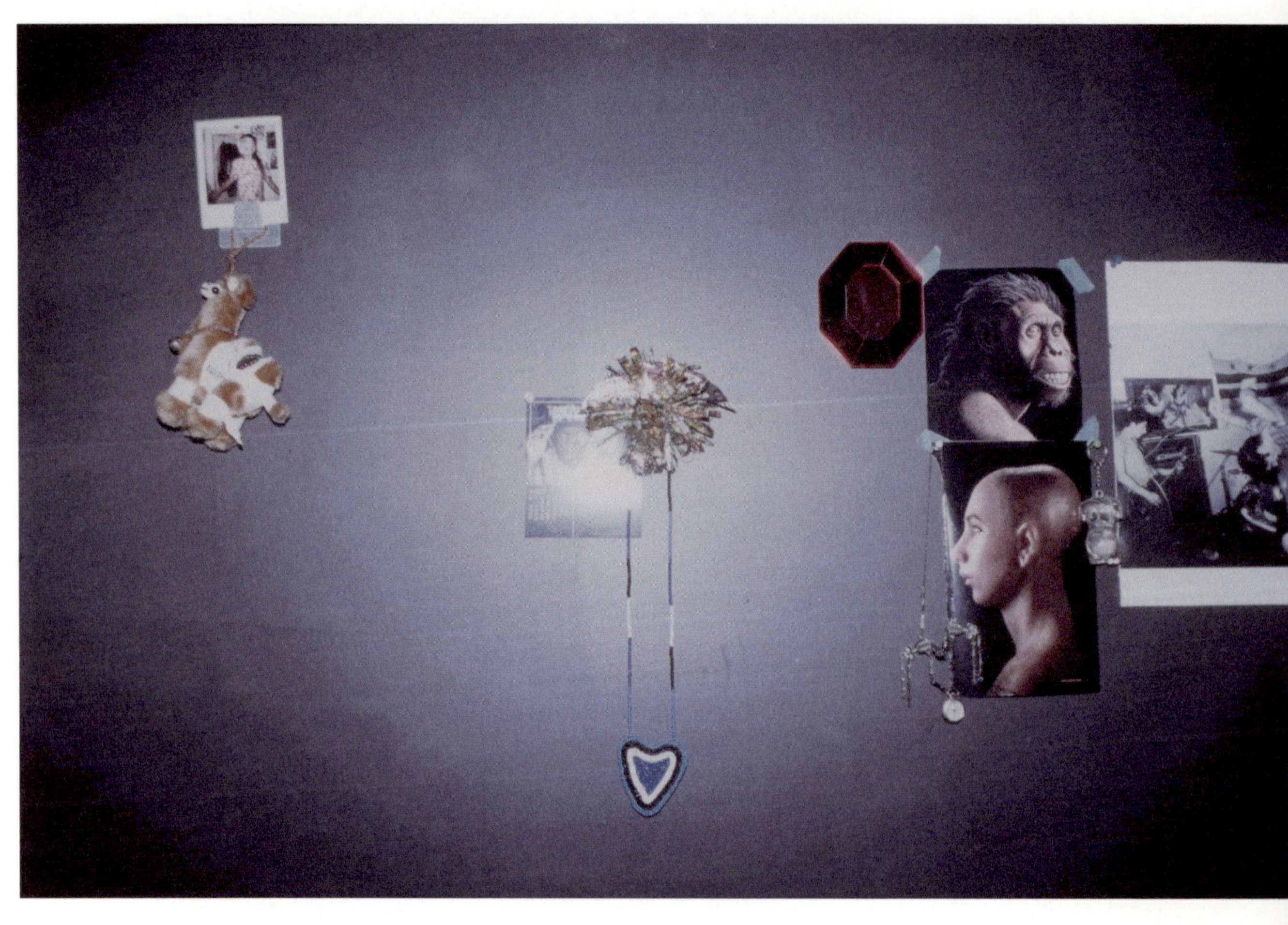

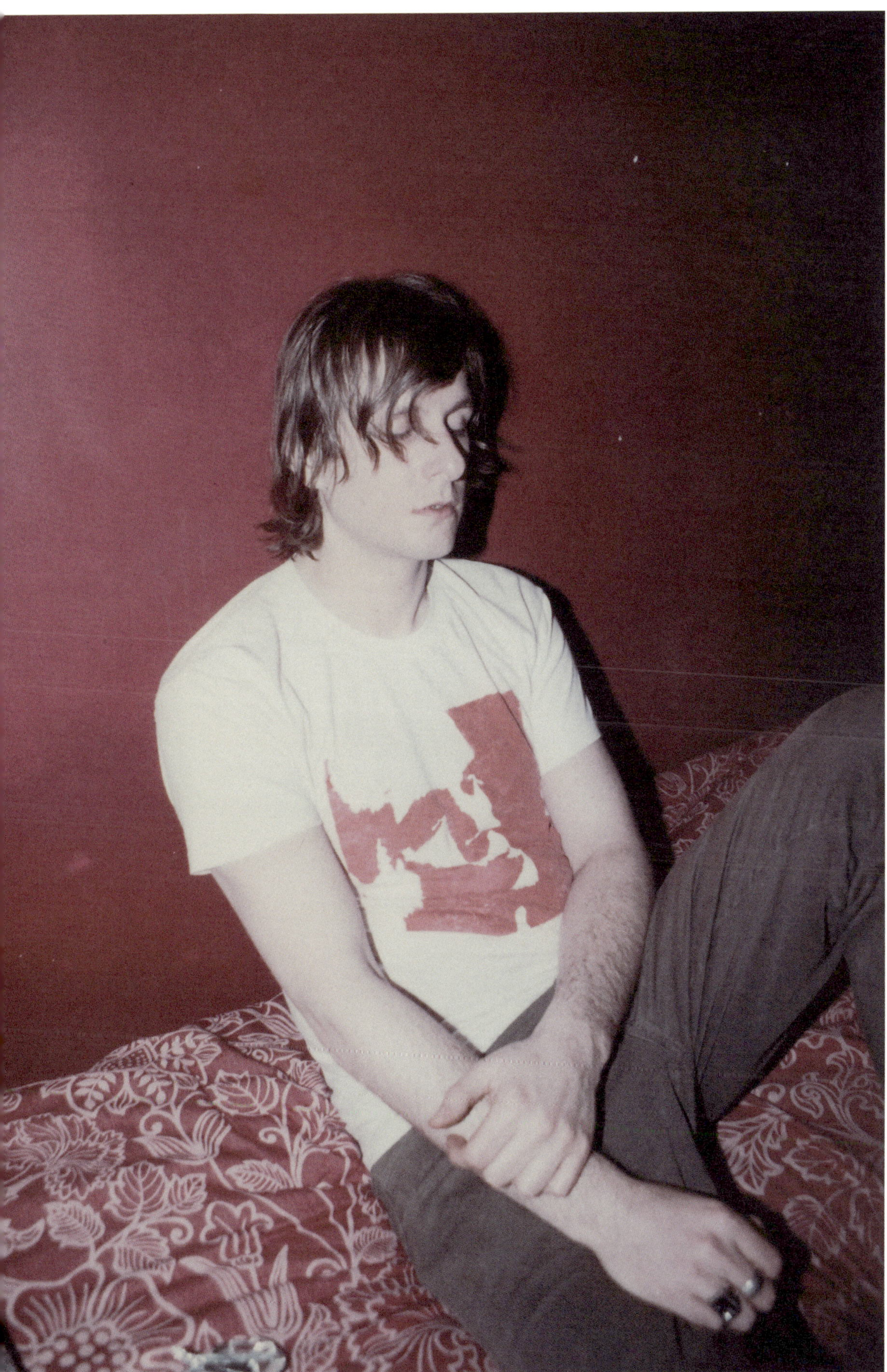

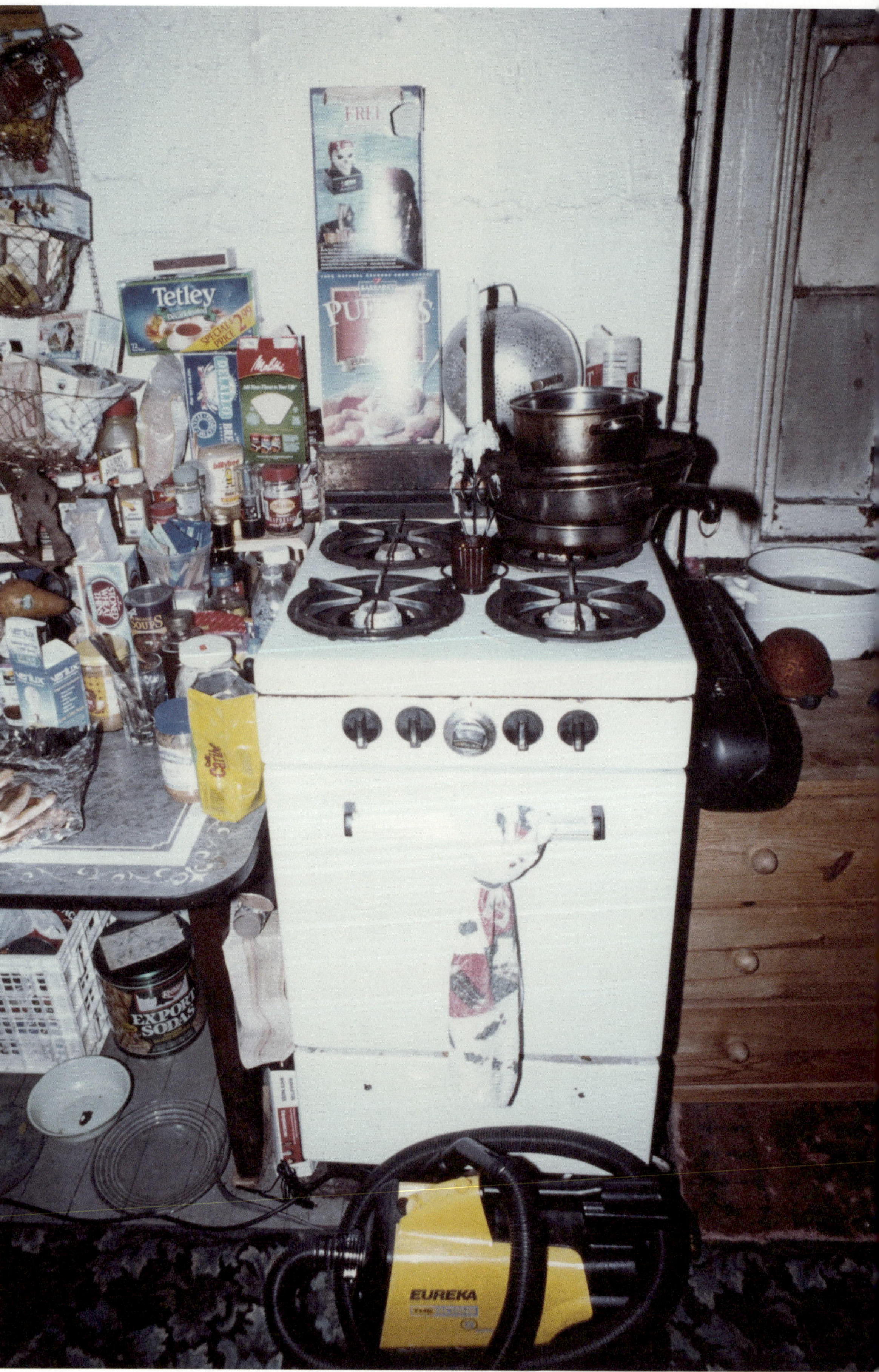
FREE
Tetley
Melitta
SOUPS
EXPORT SODAS
EUREKA

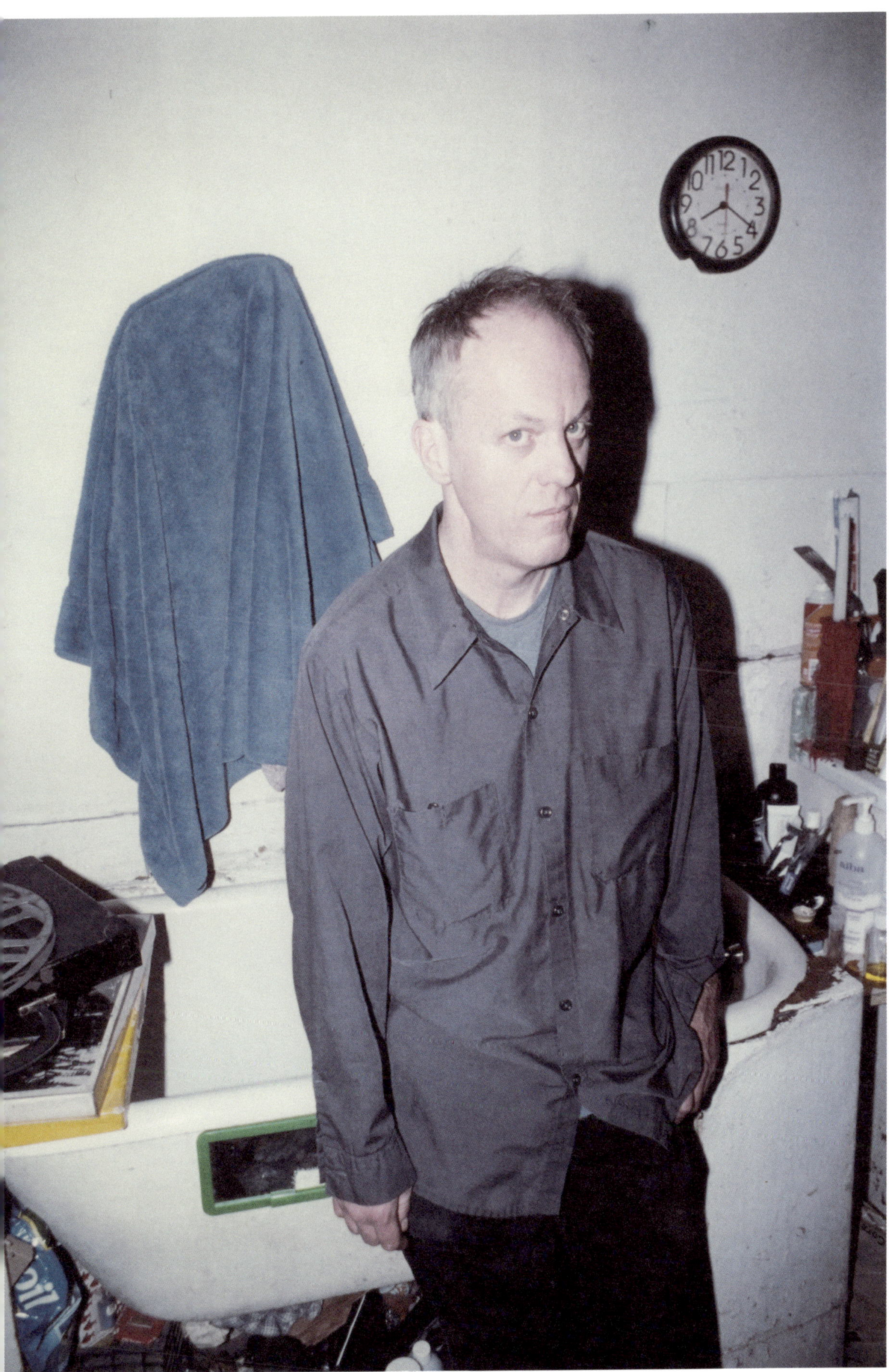

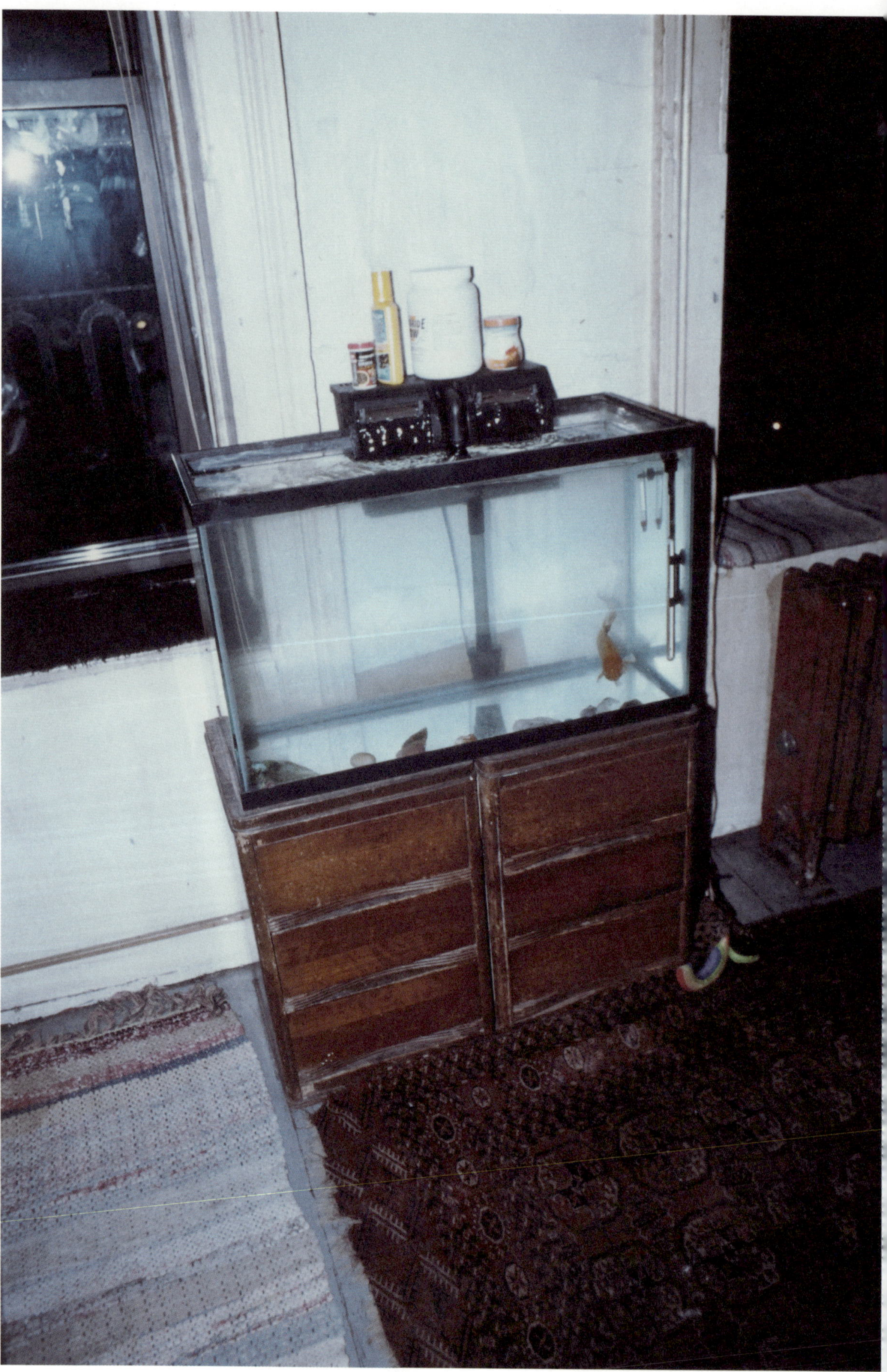

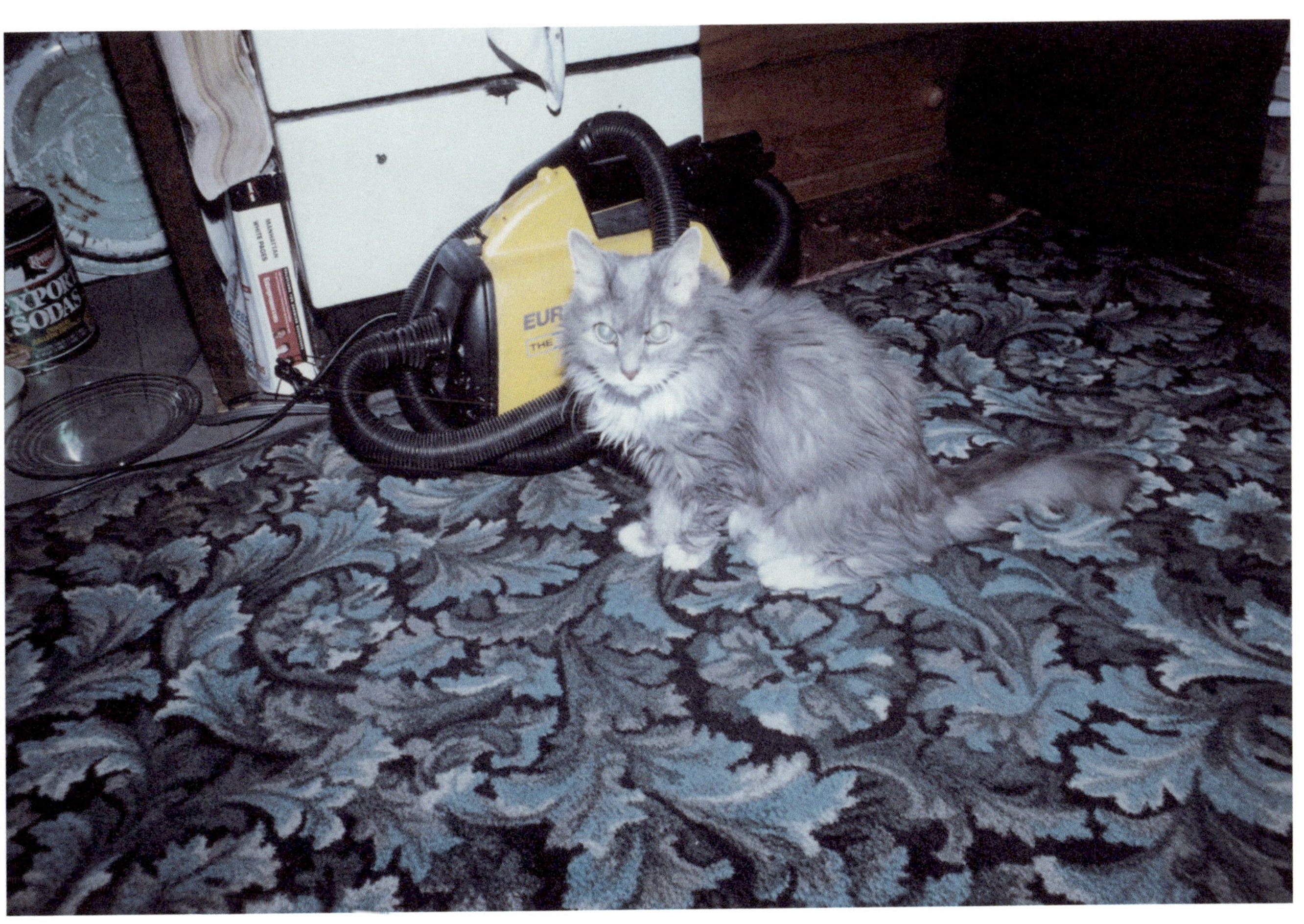
SODAS

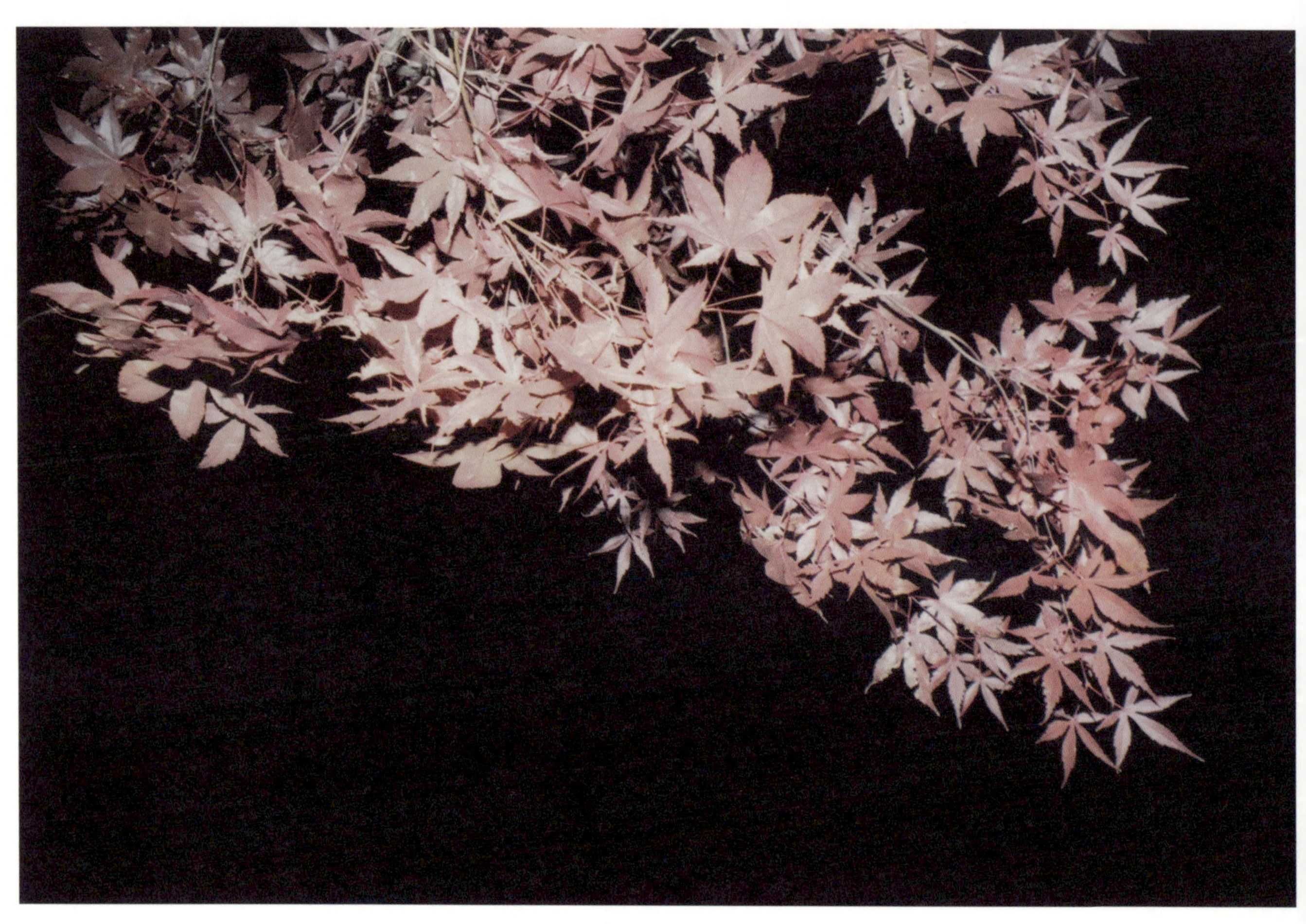

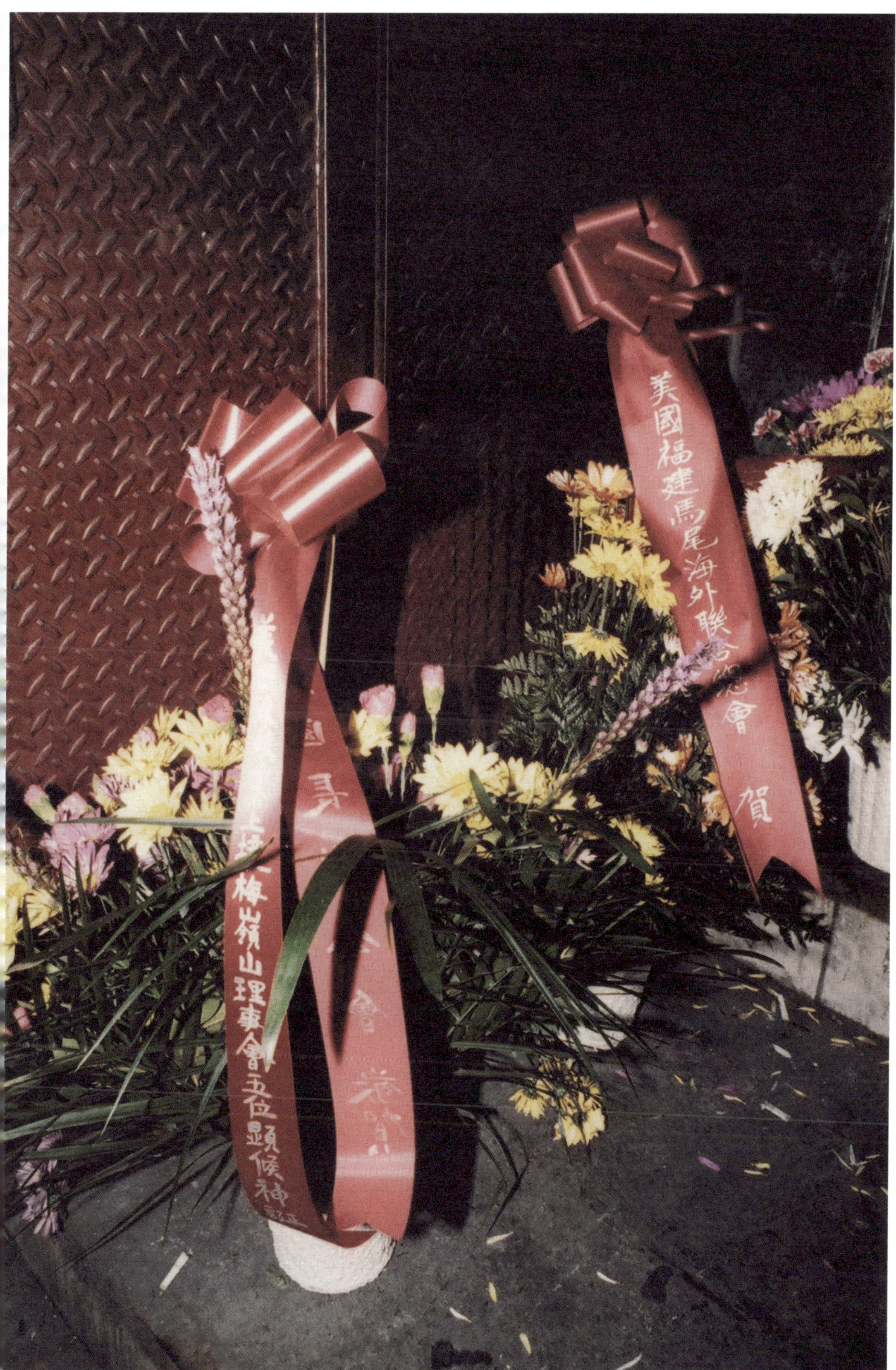
美國福建馬尾海外聯合總會
賀
梅嶺山理事會五位顯候神

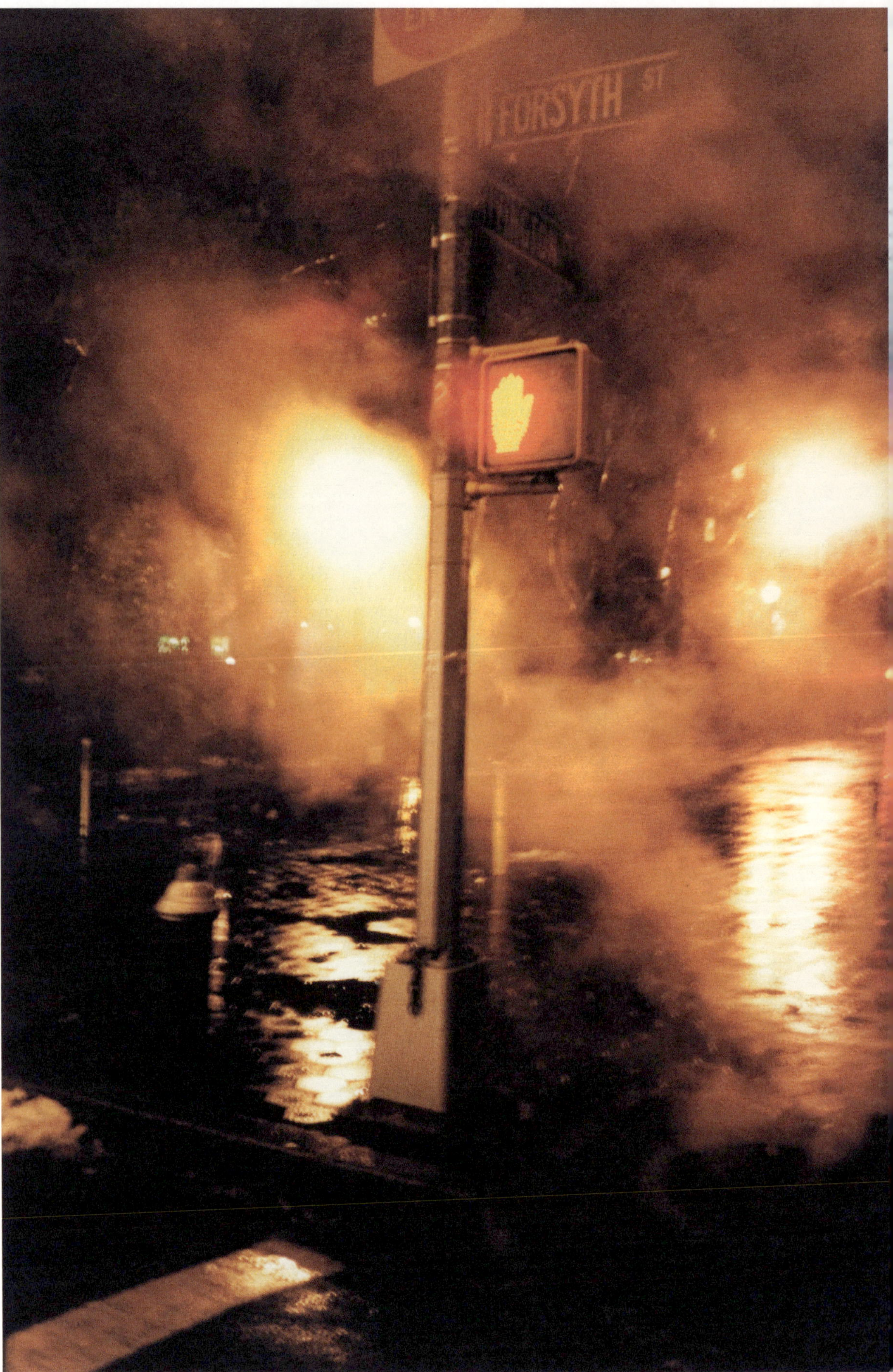
FORSYTH ST

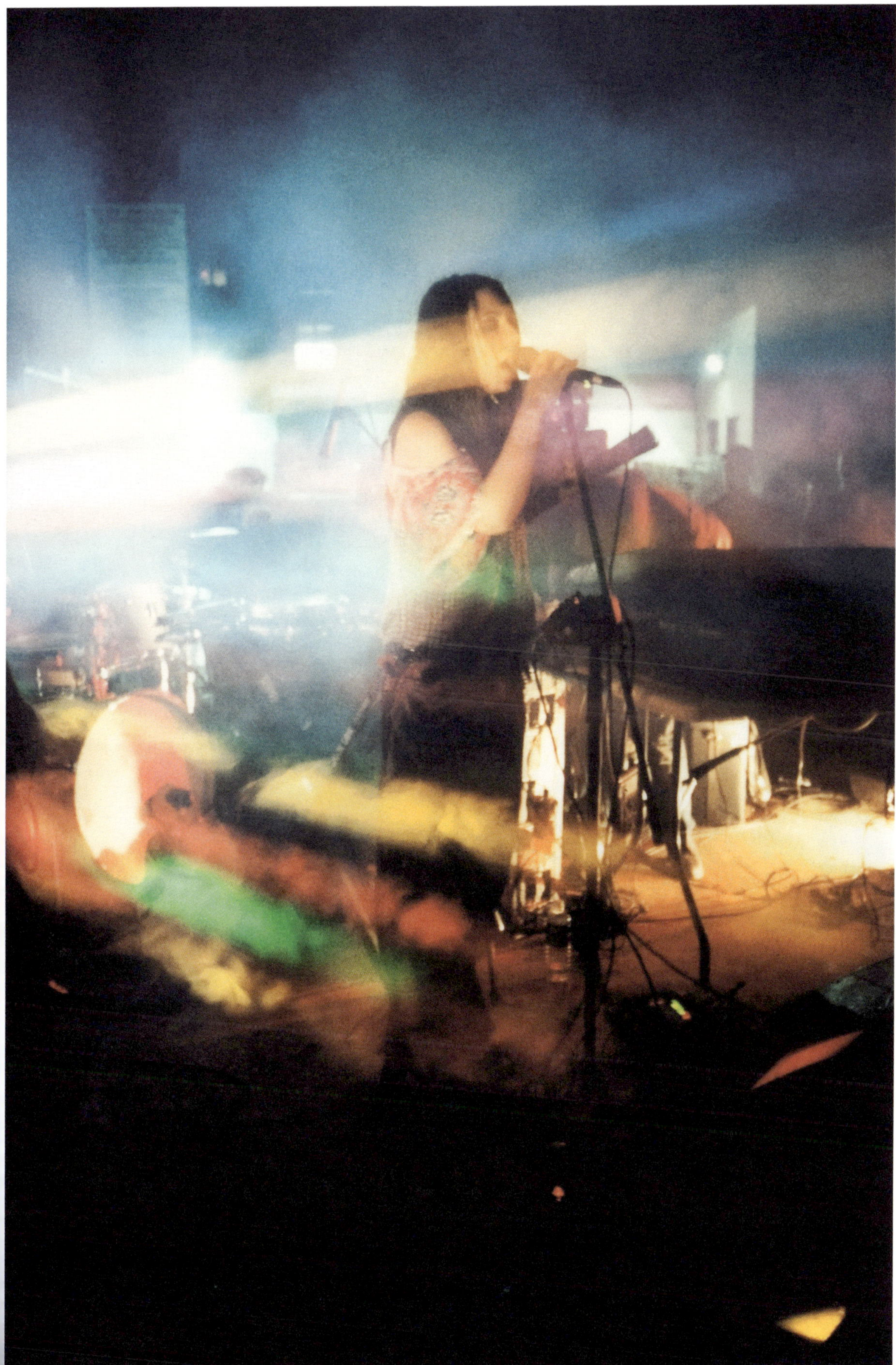

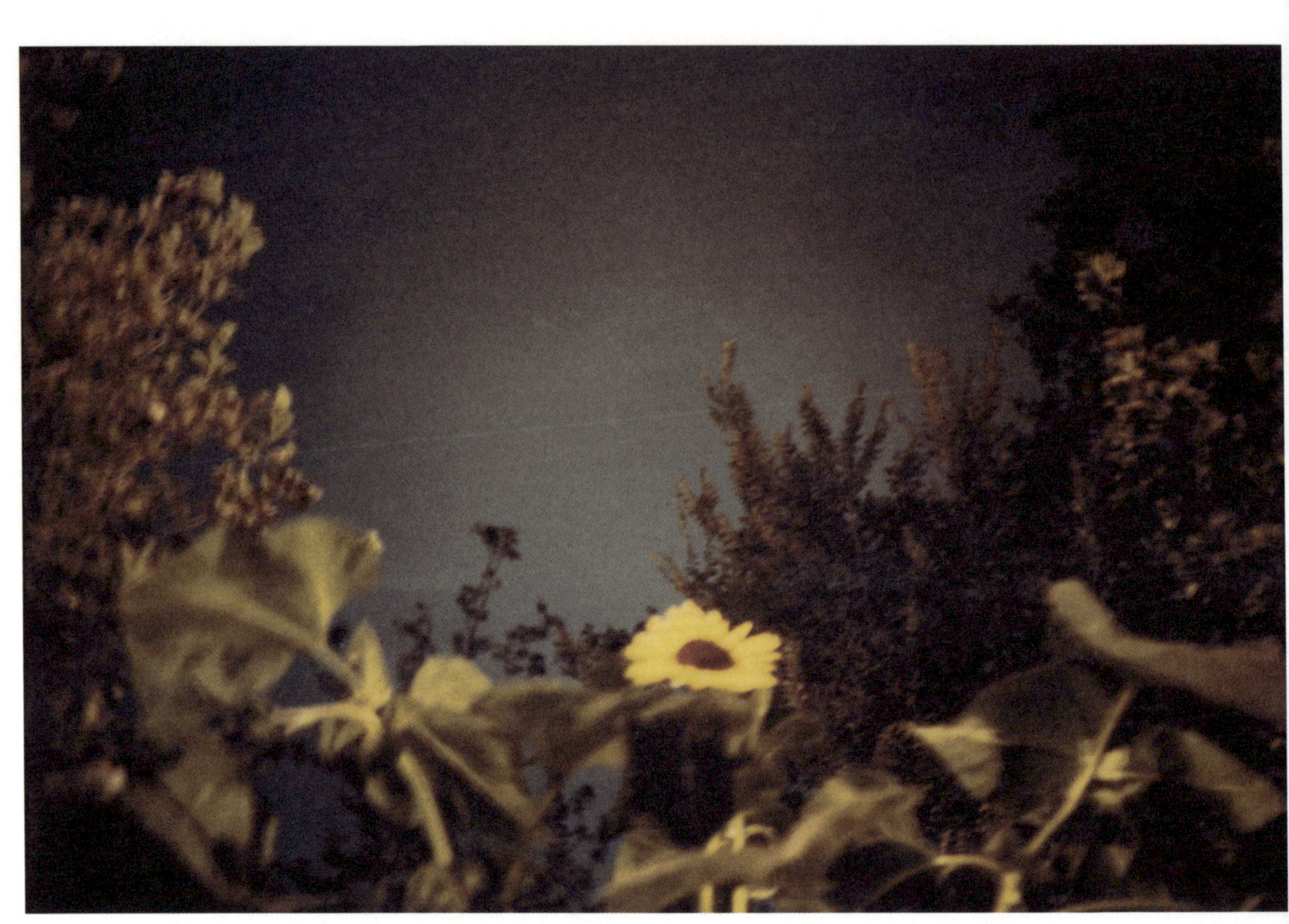

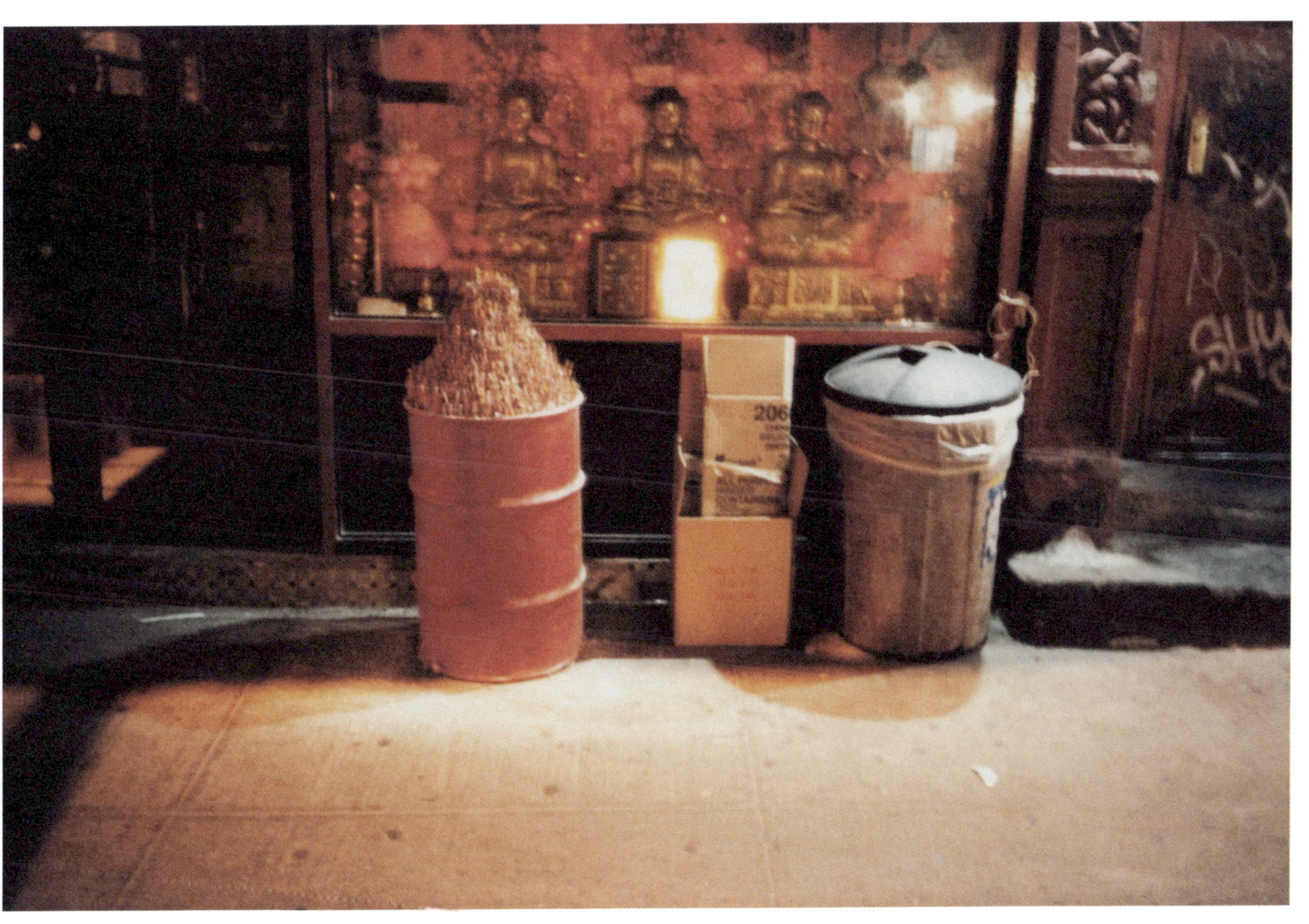
206
SHY

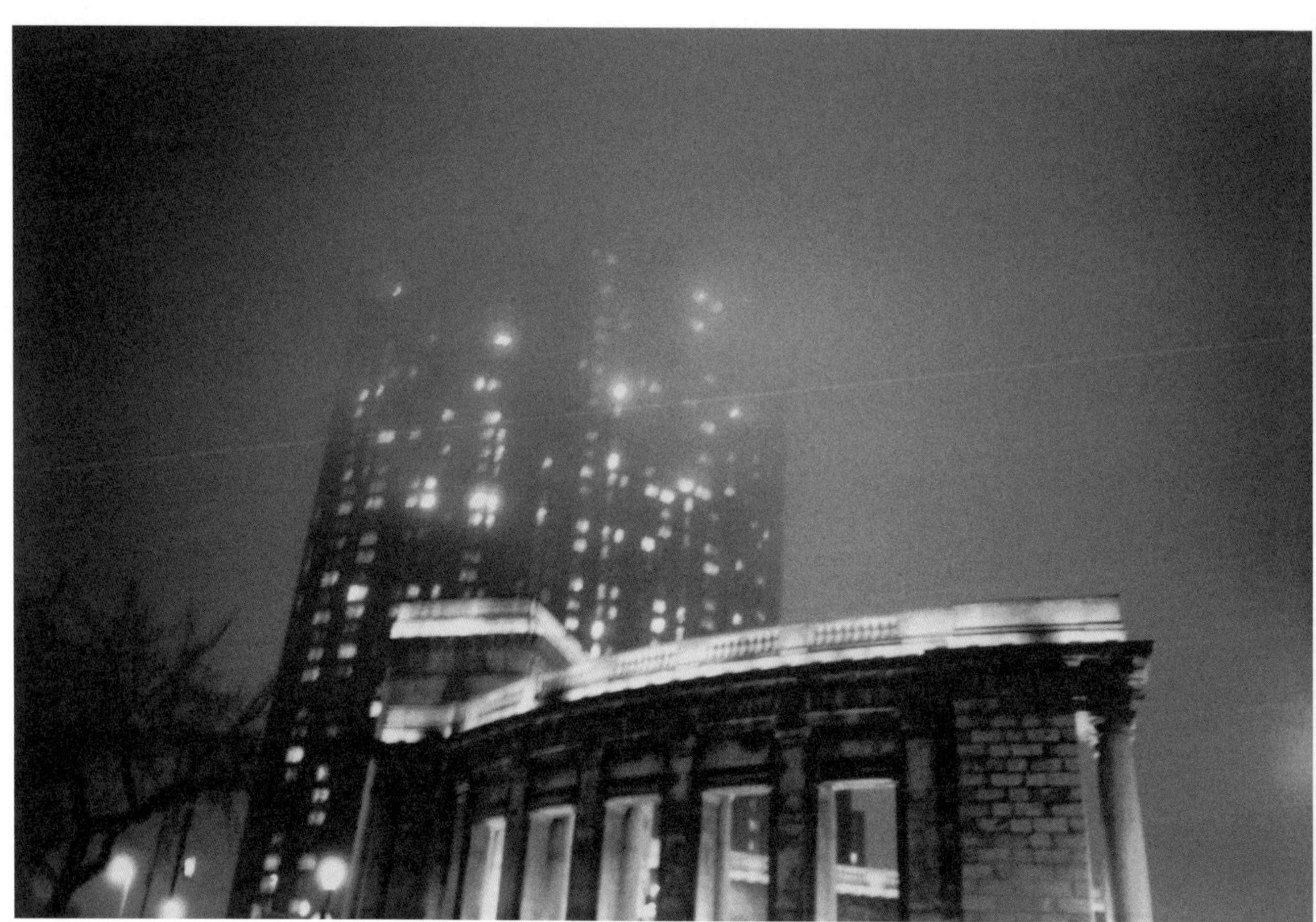

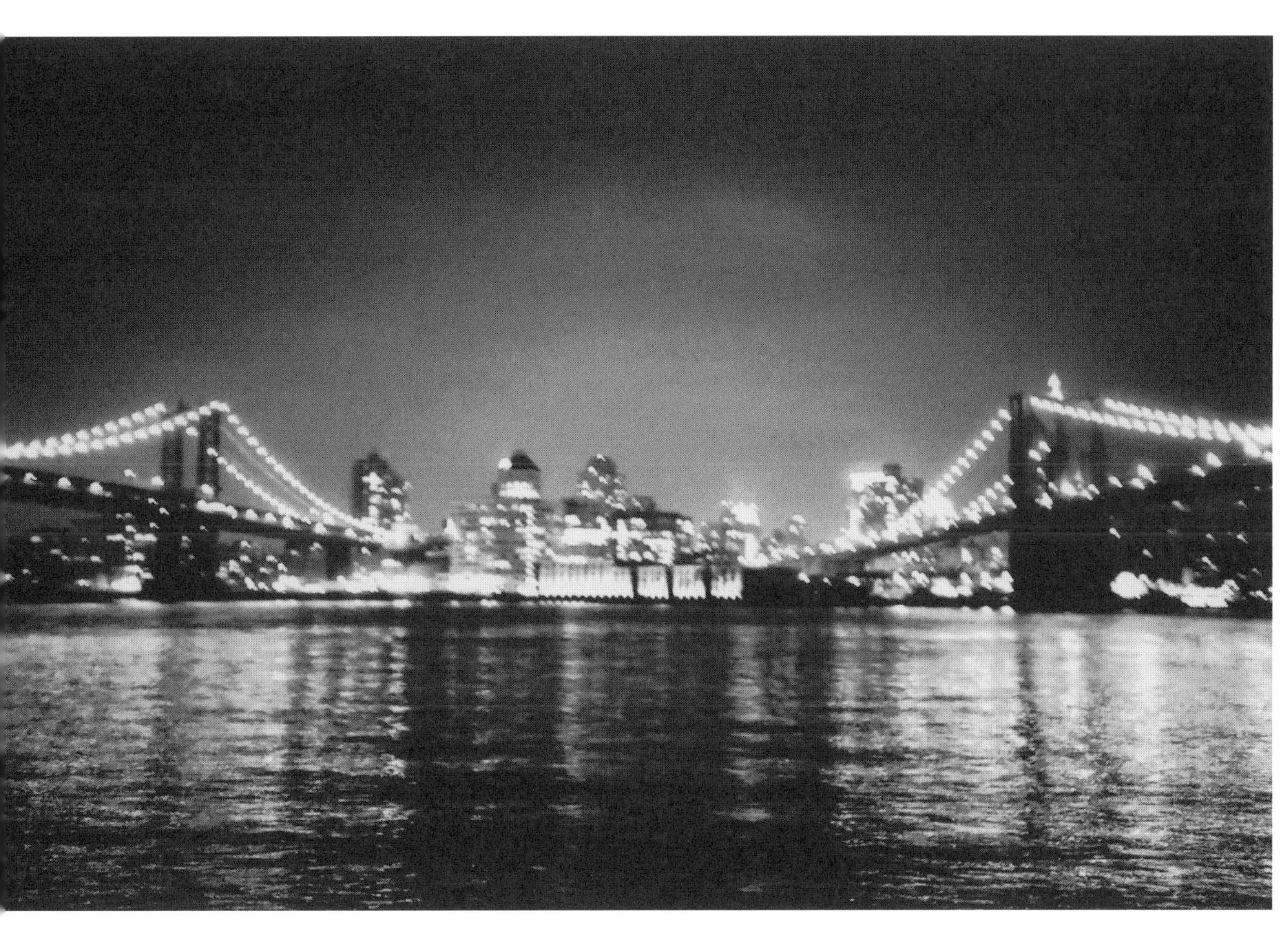

Georg Gatsas first visited our gallery at 35 Saint James Place in lower Manhattan soon after we moved in. When we met we discussed his practice and I was compelled to share with him what I was learning about the history of the neighborhood in which the gallery is located. This led him to a six month long undertaking which he eventually titled *Five Points*.

My interest in the history of lower Manhattan was inevitable because remnants of the beginnings of modern New York are evident at every turn. Despite having grown up in the city, I had somehow never been situated in a neighborhood where history was so apparent. Through this newfound interest I compiled a small library, and one book stood out as something that might interest Georg Gatsas, who was a curious Swiss artist new to the Chinatown area at that time.

He quickly connected the dots.

He realized that this very neighborhood was one of the last refuges for artists 'downtown'. His project to document artists in the neighborhoods surrounding the gallery was prescient because of its ability to place itself within the neighborhood's history, as well as the history of how it is documented. Gatsas' New York creates a trajectory of images going as far back as Jacob Riis' *How the other half lives*, whose photographs of the blight of this neighborhood (made possible by the invention of flash photography) prompted city officials to tear down most of the Five Points between 1885 and 1895.

What makes Georg Gatsas' work particularly significant is that it is a historical document. This approach puts the art back into artifact. Now we are looking at his images much in the way others must have looked at images of people in the same places over one hundred years ago. I enjoy imagining someone like Georg Gatsas in one hundred years looking at the book you are reading now, I wonder what they might have to say or might be able to learn about these places, people and things.

James Fuentes, New York City, October 2009